LEADING IMPROVEMENT IN
MATHEMATICS TEACHING AND LEARNING

LEADING IMPROVEMENT IN
MATHEMATICS TEACHING AND LEARNING

PETER SULLIVAN

Published in 2025 by Amba Press, Melbourne, Australia
www.ambapress.com.au

First published in 2020 by ACER Press, an imprint of
Australian Council for Educational Research Ltd

© Peter Sullivan 2025

This book is copyright. All rights reserved. Except under the conditions described in the *Copyright Act 1968* of Australia and subsequent amendments, and any exceptions permitted under the current statutory licence scheme administered by Copyright Agency (www.copyright.com.au), no part of this publication may be reproduced, stored in a retrieval system, transmitted, broadcast or communicated in any form or by any means, optical, digital, electronic, mechanical, photocopying, recording or otherwise, without the written permission of the publisher.

Edited by Philip Bryan
Cover design, text design and typesetting by Nada Backovic
Cover image © iStock.com/monkeybusinessimages

Paperback ISBN 9781923569140
eBook ISBN 9781923569157

A catalogue record for this book is available from the National Library of Australia.

Foreword

Research is revealing the powerful impact that school leadership teams can have in improving the quality of teaching and learning. Effective leaders create cultures of high expectations, provide clarity about what teachers are to teach and students are to learn, establish strong professional learning communities and lead ongoing efforts to improve teaching practices. (Masters 2012)

School leadership is an increasingly complex, highly demanding role. School leaders are accountable for a broad range of factors and outcomes and to a wide array of stakeholders. In establishing short- and long-term goals for improving outcomes for students, school leaders turn their minds not only to performance indicators and targets but to the methods, approaches and strategies through which those targets can be achieved.

Research tells us that schools and school systems which embrace evidence-based practice models are those most likely to achieve their goals of improving outcomes for young people. It also tells us that it is school leaders who play a critical role in identifying, implementing, embedding and leading evidence-based practice.

The 'High Impact Strategies for School Leaders' series is designed as a resource for those busy school leaders, whose ultimate aim is to improve outcomes for all learners. Each book in the series, focusing on a different domain within the school environment, unpacks for school leaders the ways high-impact strategies and practices can be applied to achieve improvement goals. Written by highly regarded experts in their fields, the 'High Impact Strategies for School Leaders' series seeks to focus attention on the role of school leaders in driving the processes that result in effective school and classroom practice and improved outcomes for students and help them navigate through the dizzying array of information about 'what works' and what doesn't.

In *Leading improvement in mathematics teaching and learning*, mathematics education expert Emeritus Professor Peter Sullivan presents a range of evidenced-informed practices that can be used as a focus for teacher professional learning and school improvement, aligning each of these with high-impact teaching strategies. Sullivan also highlights the role of principals and other school-based leaders in leading teaching and learning, and suggests that whole-school approaches are among the most successful strategies.

In his work with schools, Peter Sullivan facilitates professional learning sessions and workshops and provides support for teachers and school leadership teams. Many schools across the country have incorporated Sullivan's approaches and methods into their school improvement strategies and their classrooms, including problem-solving methods, open-ended problems, challenging tasks and task differentiation.

Sullivan draws on some of his own well-received existing approaches and the work of other educational authorities in constructing the set of seven high-impact mathematics practices that shape this book. Together, these provide an effective framework for schools and school leaders to strengthen their numeracy and mathematics teaching practices and student outcomes.

CONTENTS

Foreword		v
Introduction	**The principal as leader of teacher professional learning**	**1**
	Articulating longer term vision	3
	The theme of teacher professional learning	7
Practice 1	**Quality classroom learning experiences as a focus of teacher professional learning**	**13**
	Tasks should be challenging	18
	Choosing classroom tasks	23
	Summary and implications for professional learning	26
Practice 2	**Improving student learning by addressing the structure of lessons**	**31**
	An illustrative template for lessons focusing on understanding: Active teaching	33
	An illustrative template for lessons focusing on understanding: Purposeful games and puzzles	35

	An illustrative template for lessons focusing on problem solving: Imagined representations	38
	An illustrative template for lessons focusing on reasoning: The 'What if?' template	41
	Some elements common to each template	43
	Some elements of the 'Fractions of chocolate' lesson	46
	Summary and implications for professional learning	50
Practice 3	**The development and use of learning sequences to inform high-quality classroom learning**	**53**
	Summary and implications for professional learning	61
Practice 4	**Teacher professional learning that focuses on grouping practices**	**63**
	Accommodating the diversity of readiness in school and classroom grouping structures	67
	Ways of dealing with difference while maintaining a coherent and inclusive class community	71
	A promising approach to intervention	74
	Summary and implications for professional learning	77
Practice 5	**Teacher professional learning that focuses on classroom culture**	**79**
	Embracing challenges consistently	80
	Norms of activity	82
	Social interactions	83

	Summary and implications for professional learning	84
Practice 6	**Improving learning through supported collaborative planning processes**	**87**
	Planning assumptions	88
	Collaborative planning informed by research	89
	Summary and implications for professional learning	94
Practice 7	**Professional learning focusing on six principles of effective mathematics teaching**	**97**
	Principle 1: Setting goals	98
	Principle 2: Making connections	100
	Principle 3: Fostering engagement	102
	Principle 4: Differentiating challenges	103
	Principle 5: Structuring lessons	104
	Principle 6: Promoting fluency and transfer	106
	Summary and implications for professional learning	107
Conclusion		**109**
References		**113**

INTRODUCTION

The principal as leader of teacher professional learning

Leading improvement in mathematics teaching and learning is intended to inform approaches to improving planning and teaching mathematics in Australian schools, which will, in turn, improve student learning. The intent is to inform the development of school-based improvement plans and targets. Each chapter explains and presents arguments for recommended strategies and their likely impact.

The word *improving* has been chosen deliberately. There are many schools that are already meeting the needs of most of their students, and there are many outstanding teachers. In such schools and classrooms there is limited imperative to 'change'. But everyone can improve, even schools and teachers that are already high performers.

An underlying assumption is that this 'improvement' can be led by the school leadership team, and especially the school principal—particularly in schools and classrooms that are not currently serving the needs of most of their students. Although some schools and teachers manage to improve even when principals focus on other aspects of their roles than leading teaching and learning, the strategies for improvement are complex and multi-faceted, and whole-school approaches that build on specific and articulated plans are more likely to be successful. The focus of this book is to provide details for a set of strategies that individually and together can be the focus of teacher professional learning and school improvement.

A further assumption is that edicts and compliance targets are unlikely to elicit teacher commitment to the type of long-term improvement initiatives that are necessary. Although there is a need to collaboratively develop goals and processes for improvement, teacher professional learning must be at the centre of any improvement initiative. It can be taken as a given that all teachers already teach as well as they can, so improvement must be driven by new teacher knowledge and attitudes. In other words, learning improvement is connected to teaching improvement.

This book should be read in conjunction with Sullivan's *Teaching mathematics: using research-informed strategies* (2011), which outlines research-informed approaches to teaching mathematics, some of which are elaborated here. Further key ideas that can be found in Sullivan (2011) include:

> Section 2, which elaborates the curriculum goals of mathematics

> Section 3, which summarises findings from international and national assessments

> Section 4, which explains the distinction between mathematics and numeracy.

Note that throughout this book, the word *mathematics* includes everything encompassed by both 'mathematics' and 'numeracy'.

Articulating longer term vision

Before elaborating upon the specific improvement strategies, the following describes some thinking about the broader goals of education. It would not make sense to have one vision for education generally, while having mathematics curriculum and pedagogies that conflict with that vision. Likewise, it would be unnecessarily limiting to restrict measures of improvement to increases in student scores on normed assessments or national assessments generally.

The directions and emphases of a possible vision can be guided by a major report anticipating and setting goals for 21st-century learners. The Organisation for Economic Co-operation and Development (OECD 2019) proposes aspirations for education globally in the year 2030. It also outlines specific goals of education—two of which are particularly relevant for the teaching of mathematics.

The first goal is to maximise career and life opportunities of all learners, which implies the centrality of inclusive approaches to planning and teaching. The OECD articulates this vision as follows:

> *We are committed to helping every learner develop as a whole person, fulfil his or her potential and help shape a shared future built on the well-being of individuals, communities and the planet.* (OECD 2019)

The key word in this statement is *every*. Assuming that schools also incorporate such aspirations into their visions, there is a need to examine pedagogies—especially classroom organisation and grouping structures—to ensure that opportunities for learning are available for all students.

This is particularly relevant for mathematics teaching, as some schools group students so that various subgroups experience different curriculum content. What is concerning is that the limited content and pedagogy these students experience can mean that they fall further and further behind—and become progressively unable to take advantage of the opportunities that mathematics offers in terms of study and careers. Stratification of opportunity comes with risks that are contrary to the inclusive goals of education. This book argues that approaches that maximise opportunities for all students are not only desirable, but possible.

The second goal is preparing students for uncertain and volatile futures, implying that capabilities for independent thinking and creativity can be fostered through education. The OECD elaborates this vision as follows:

> [Students] will need to be responsible and empowered, placing collaboration above division, and sustainability above short-term gain. In the face of an increasingly volatile, uncertain, complex and ambiguous world, education can make the difference as to whether people embrace the challenges they are confronted with or whether they are defeated by them. And in an era characterised by a new explosion of scientific knowledge and a growing array of complex societal problems, it is appropriate that curricula should continue to evolve, perhaps in radical ways. (OECD 2019)

As an example of a threat to this goal, there are schools and teachers that adopt pedagogies that put the teacher at the centre. Many of their lessons start with the teacher explaining what students need to do, after which students practise what they have been told.

The risk with such approaches is twofold. First, students become reliant on the teacher for their learning, and develop a dependent self-concept. Second, students come to see mathematics as something that is 'told' or 'given' to them, rather than mathematics presenting different ways of thinking about and describing the world. The argument is that all students benefit by engaging with mathematics for themselves—generally prior to teacher instruction—and through this engagement they become more adaptable and better able to cope with uncertainty and complexity, and to think for themselves.

In this book, I argue that both of these goals are different from common approaches to mathematics teaching in some schools in Australia. If this is true, then improvement is needed—and this improvement is best driven by school-based leaders. It also emphasises the importance of having a vision and making sure that it is in alignment with classroom practices.

The OECD vision emphasises the active role of the learner and future citizen in creating knowledge and making decisions, as well as the need for education to foster risk-taking and autonomous thinking. Based on its vision, the OECD articulates 'design principles' for changes in curricula that can inform school-based improvement initiatives. In terms of concepts, content and topic design, the OECD summarises the characteristics of effective curriculums as follows:

> **Student agency**: *The curriculum should be designed around students to motivate them and recognise their prior knowledge, skills, attitudes and values.*

> **Rigour**: *Topics should be challenging and enable deep thinking and reflection.*

> **Focus**: *A relatively small number of topics should be introduced in each grade to ensure the depth and quality of students' learning. Topics may overlap in order to reinforce key concepts.*

> **Coherence**: *Topics should be sequenced to reflect the logic of the academic discipline or disciplines upon which they draw, enabling progression from basic to more advanced concepts through stages and age levels.*

> **Alignment**: *The curriculum should be well aligned with teaching and assessment practices. While the technologies to assess many of the desired outcomes do not yet exist, different assessment practices might be needed for different purposes.*

> *New assessment methods should be developed that value student outcomes and actions that cannot always be measured.*

> › **Transferability**: *Higher priority should be given to knowledge, skills, attitudes and values that can be learned in one context and transferred to others.*

> › **Choice**: *Students should be offered a diverse range of topic and project options, and the opportunity to suggest their own topics and projects, with the support to make well-informed choices.* (OECD 2019)

School-based curriculum initiatives also need a similar set of principles to guide development. The final section of *Leading improvement in mathematics teaching and learning* refers back to these principles. The OECD goes on to propose processes by which such curriculums might be designed:

> › **Teacher agency**: *Teachers should be empowered to use their professional knowledge, skills and expertise to deliver the curriculum effectively.*

> › **Authenticity**: *Learners should be able to link their learning experiences to the real world and have a sense of purpose in their learning. This requires interdisciplinary and collaborative learning alongside mastery of discipline-based knowledge.*

> › **Interrelation**: *Learners should be given opportunities to discover how a topic or concept can link and connect to other topics or concepts within and across disciplines, and with real life outside of school.*

> › **Flexibility**: *The concept of curriculum should be developed from 'predetermined and static' to 'adaptable and dynamic'. Schools and teachers should be able to update and align the curriculum to reflect evolving societal requirements, as well as individual learning needs.*

> **Engagement**. *Teachers, students and other relevant stakeholders should be involved early in the development of the curriculum to ensure their ownership for implementation. (OECD 2019)*

These processes can inform school-based professional learning. It is worth pointing out that the OECD has built its policy around findings from large-scale data, both from the Program of International Student Assessment (PISA 2018), and other economic and social research. This book, rather than justifying any of these principles, elaborates why mathematics teaching can seek to incorporate such approaches into planning and teaching, and how school principals and other school-based leaders can foster and support the improvement in practice that may be necessary.

The theme of teacher professional learning

The overall theme of this book is structured teacher learning, and I will elaborate on a range of practices that can be the focus of policy development and collaborative initiatives. In particular, even though the goal is improvement in students' achievement and engagement when learning mathematics, the sections are written to inform professional learning for teachers.

The intention is that principals and nominated leaders will lead the professional learning. Each practice that forms a section of this book is connected explicitly to the High Impact Teaching Strategies (HITS) (Department of Education and Training 2017). The HITS were developed in Victoria, although similar concepts can be found across other jurisdictions. Table 1 lists the practices and their connected HITS. Many of the practices use a number of the strategies, but only the most relevant strategies have been listed.

Table 1: The connections between the practices advocated and the High Impact Teaching Strategies (HITS)

HITS	PRACTICE
Setting goals	1: Quality classroom learning experiences as a focus of teacher professional learning
Structuring lessons	2: Improving student learning by addressing the structure of lessons
Explicit teaching	2: Improving student learning by addressing the structure of lessons
Worked examples	2: Improving student learning by addressing the structure of lessons
Collaborative learning	7: Professional learning focusing on six principles of effective mathematics teaching
Multiple exposures	3: The development and use of learning sequences to inform high-quality classroom learning
Questioning	2: Improving student learning by addressing the structure of lessons
Feedback	2: Improving student learning by addressing the structure of lessons
Metacognitive strategies	3: The development and use of learning sequences to inform high-quality classroom learning
Differentiated teaching	4: Teacher professional learning that focuses on grouping practices

Although the HITS relate explicitly to aspects of teaching, there are two practices that are more general. They are:

> Practice 5: Teacher professional learning that focuses on classroom culture

> Practice 6: Improving learning through supported collaborative planning processes.

The various suggestions for professional learning and teaching practice are based on beliefs that:

> all students can learn mathematics—although this happens at different rates, and in different ways

> all students can benefit from learning mathematics to prepare them for active citizenship, career opportunities, further study and enjoyment of mathematical ways of seeing the world

> although many common teaching practices are effective, in general, 'more of the same' will not effect improvement, and so an expectation of and support for experimentation and reflection should inform school-based initiatives

> change in teaching and learning takes time—some changes are more amenable to teachers than others, and there are no 'quick fixes'

> there is no one way to improve the experience of all students, so the ideal mathematics programs and pedagogies will incorporate a 'balanced diet' of approaches.

Each section includes specific suggestions for actions that aim to stimulate improvement. The discussion draws on examples and arguments that are equally relevant for primary and secondary teachers of mathematics. Where examples are used, they are mainly from upper primary and junior secondary levels.

While any one of these sections can productively be the focus of individual professional learning sessions, effective mathematics teaching involves combining them all. For this reason, I recommend that leaders engage with the whole book rather than individual sections. However, there is a caveat: as planning for improvement within a school builds on current approaches and what teachers already know and believe, the improvement goals may need to be pursued in stages, possibly over several years.

Sullivan, Borcek, Walker and Rennie (2016) describe the interaction of factors influencing planning and teaching of mathematics. They connect three nodes with each other, specifically:

> teachers' knowledge of mathematics and pedagogy
> teachers' beliefs, values and attitudes
> opportunities and constraints that teachers anticipate experiencing.

Each node informs teachers' planning intentions and their classroom actions. Then, in turn, the actions taken impact on each node. In other words, the model indicates that what teachers know, their dispositions, and their anticipation of barriers they may experience influence their planning, and this in turn informs what happens in the classroom, which then influences each of the other factors the next time around.

All professional learning should address each node. In other words, it is not enough to focus just on knowledge, or just on beliefs, but ideally these should be connected. Likewise, the constraints should be considered at the same time, along with the implications for planning and assessment. This model of factors informs the discussion throughout this book, and is also addressed in the conclusion.

PRACTICE 1

Quality classroom learning experiences as a focus of teacher professional learning

Improving students' experiences with mathematics in the classroom will directly lead to greater engagement in learning, and to gains in achievement measures. Because learning experiences are chosen and implemented by teachers, the quality of classroom experiences can productively be the focus of teacher professional learning.

The roles of school-based leaders are critical, and these include fostering an interest in quality experiences, as well as supporting improvement in an ongoing way. This practice is discussed first, as all of the other practices elaborated in this book assume quality learning experiences.

In Practice 1, and in the practices that follow, I use specific examples to elaborate on the point being made. However, my use of examples does not reduce the generality of the recommendations—

and I am not proposing that they form the content of specific professional learning sessions. The terms 'learning experiences' and 'tasks' are used interchangeably.

Practice 1 is informed by the perspective that learning is optimally activated by having students engage in tasks or learning experiences that have been thoughtfully chosen by their teachers—rather than having explanations given to them by their teachers. More than any other action that teachers may take, posing rich tasks that engage students in thinking for themselves about mathematics is the main stimulus for student learning (Anthony & Walshaw 2009).

A quick note about the terminology used. Drawing on Watson and Sullivan (2008):

> *Task* refers to information that serves as the prompt for student work, and provides the starting point and the context for their learning—i.e. questions, situations and instructions.

> *Activity* refers to the thoughts and actions that students take in response to the task—e.g. physical, spoken, written or recorded responses.

It follows that an important focus of professional learning for teachers of mathematics is the types of tasks that can be posed to elicit student learning. However, a key issue is that different types of tasks have different purposes, and the optimal approaches can be described using the metaphor of a 'balanced diet', in which each food group contributes to the whole.

An emphasis on the characteristics and potential of tasks can:

> provide a language and focus for specific professional learning sessions

> form part of team-planning meetings

> form the basis of lesson observations.

This emphasis can also inform resource purchases and school-based processes for curating documents and materials, including those created in the school.

The following draws on an article by Watson and Sullivan (2008), in turn building on Sullivan (2007), which argues that a focus on classroom tasks as part of professional learning can:

> - inform teachers about the range and purpose of possible student learning experiences
>
> - provide opportunities for teachers to learn more about mathematics
>
> - provide insight into the nature of mathematical activity
>
> - stimulate and inform teachers' theorising about students' learning.

Stein, Grover, and Henningsen (1996) explain that consideration of mathematical classroom tasks by teachers goes from the:

1. task as presented in instructional materials or teacher's resources, to the …

2. task as intended by the teacher in the classroom, to the …

3. task as experienced by students, which creates the potential for …

4. students' learning.

The focus in Practice 1 is on Step 1 and Step 2—specifically, the teacher's choice of tasks selected and adapted from available resources, the use of tasks to create lessons (see Practice 2), and the intention to plan sequences of lessons (see Practice 3).

Of course, the choice of a task—and its inclusion in a lesson—does not automatically ensure student learning. Central to the effective choice and use of tasks is what the teacher sees as the mathematics to be learned, and the way that mathematics is learned.

Since much mathematics is abstract, even in the early years, it does not make sense to start with the teacher explaining the abstraction. It is preferable for students to have a relevant experience first, so that the concepts are more real, tangible and imaginable.

To give a specific example, the idea that we can calculate 32 + 10 by adding one 10, rather than 10 ones, is abstract. It is preferable for students to engage in activities where the possibility of adding one 10 emerges. So it is not enough for teachers to tell students a rule. Students can be engaged in thinking about the advantages of adding one 10, the various ways that adding one 10 can be modelled and patterns that can be seen in the hundreds number chart. Note that the intention is that students can generalise learning to add one 10 to all possible examples (within their number range). So the goal of learning is not finding the solution for a specific question, but for students to be able to add 10 to any number.

In almost all cases, the general rule of 'experience before instruction' applies in the case of mathematics learning. That is, students will ideally engage in problem-type experiences that alert them to the possibility of adding one 10, which can then be discussed and the teacher can elaborate ways in which the learning is applicable across various similar situations.

This approach can generally be described as structured inquiry. In a 2011 meta-analysis of 164 studies, Alfieri, Brooks, Aldrich and Tenenbaum distinguished between structured inquiry-based approaches and unstructured inquiry-based approaches. They found that unstructured inquiry was inferior to more explicit instructional approaches in terms of its impact on assessed student learning, whereas structured inquiry was superior to all other instructional approaches. They argue that:

> *participation in guided discovery is better for learners than being provided with an explanation or explicitly taught how to succeed on a task.* (p. 11)

The choice of task is particularly informed by perspectives on curriculum. While many texts and teaching approaches emphasise the development of efficiency with procedures, the Australian Curriculum: Mathematics draws on strands of mathematical learning articulated by Kilpatrick, Swafford and Findell (2001) to describe the focus on mathematical learning as:

> understanding
> - comprehension of mathematical concepts, operations, and relations

> fluency
> - skill in carrying out procedures flexibly, accurately, efficiently and appropriately, and, in addition to these procedures, factual knowledge and concepts that come to mind readily

> problem solving
> - experience in formulating, representing and solving mathematical problems

> reasoning
> - capacity for logical thought, reflection, explanation and justification.

Kilpatrick et al. (2001) also describe a fifth aspect named 'productive disposition', which they interpret as the inclination to see mathematics as sensible, useful and worthwhile, coupled with an appreciation of diligence, persistence and the individual's own efficacy. It is assumed that all classroom tasks will seek to develop this productive disposition, which also connects to the other four proficiencies.

It is common for teachers of mathematics to start learning sequences by emphasising understanding and fostering fluency, and then to pose problems and encourage reasoning subsequently. As part of a balanced diet, it is also arguable that there are advantages—

at least some of the time—in engaging students with one or more concepts by posing problems and encouraging them to reason, which in turn helps to build understanding and leads to fluency.

A particular emphasis in professional learning related to choice and potential of classroom tasks is the extent to which productively challenging tasks are more effective for engaging students in building knowledge of mathematics for themselves than are tasks that are simple. Approaches in many textbooks seem to assume that students should work on easy tasks, with the rationale presumably being that success at easy tasks builds students' confidence. For example, the ICE–EM series (2019) starts the Year 7 chapter on solving equations with exercises like $x + 3 = 5$. The texts then proceed to pose identical questions in the corresponding chapters in Years 8 and 9. It did make me wonder what students in Year 9 think when they are asked to engage with such trivial exercises for the third straight year. It is difficult to imagine that the exercises will engage their brains.

Tasks should be challenging

Learning is most effective when students are engaged in higher order thinking as they work on tasks appropriately challenging for them. The following discussion draws on Sullivan, Bobis, Downton, Hughes, Livy, McCormick and Russo (2020). A task or problem is considered to be challenging if students do not initially know how to proceed, have not been told the steps by the teacher, and are expected to make decisions on solutions or solution strategies for themselves.

Consider these two scenarios:

Scenario 1: Some lessons proceed from simple to complex. This results in students beginning lessons knowing what to do and—since the examples are presented in the order simple to complex—eventually arriving at the end of the lesson just having reached a more complex task they cannot solve. As a result, the students feel they have regressed from knowing to not knowing. This is the exact opposite of learning.

Scenario 2: An alternate approach is when lessons start with students encountering tasks for which they do not (yet) know what to do. Lessons are structured so that students come to know what to do (see Practice 2 and Practice 6). In these lessons, students feel they have moved from not knowing to knowing. That is learning.

Of course, engagement with challenge needs to be productive. A common metaphor is the 'zone of proximal development' (Vygotsky 1978) for the student, which is described as the:

> *distance between the actual developmental level as determined by independent problem solving and the level of potential development as determined by problem solving under adult guidance or in collaboration with more capable peers. (p. 86)*

Various sections of this book address the issue of 'adult guidance'. Many mathematics concepts are difficult to understand—at least initially—and students benefit when they persist with concepts and tasks that include:

> concentrating
> applying themselves
> believing they can succeed

> connecting effort with learning.

Tasks designed to foster such actions are termed 'challenging', because they allow for the possibility of sustained thinking, decision-making and some risk-taking by students. As Wiliam (2016), citing Daniel Willingham, writes:

> *Students remember what they have been thinking about, so if you make the learning too easy, students don't have to work hard to make sense of what they are learning and, as a result, forget it quickly.*

In other words, students are more likely to make sense of mathematics and remember what they have learned if they work on tasks that are appropriately challenging. The OECD (2016) uses the term 'cognitive activation' to describe such challenges, and refers to the benefits of posing tasks that take time, for which the solution path is not obvious, and which create opportunities for students to learn from their mistakes. Based on analysis of results from PISA, the OECD argues that 'cognitive-activation instruction is associated with a 19-point increase in mathematics score across OECD countries, after accounting for other teaching strategies' (OECD 2016, Figure 2.2).

Christiansen and Walther (1986) argue that the interplay between different aspects of learning inherent in 'non-routine tasks'—so-called because the solution is not solved by a routine known to the students—provide ideal conditions for cognitive development because:

> the new knowledge is constructed relationally

> items of earlier knowledge are activated and consolidated.

One of teachers' frequently expressed concerns is that students are motivated by success, yet teachers see the need for that success as contradictory to the notion of challenge. However, Middleton (1995) explains that although students are indeed motivated by success, these successes need to be genuine, not merely the completion of simple tasks. More important for students' motivation is what Middleton terms 'control'. This is interpreted as students making their own choices about the type of solution or solution strategies they use when solving tasks. In fact, it is arguable that engagement is more a product of such control than it is of perceived relevance.

Connected to this notion of challenge is ensuring that the cognitive load of a task is intrinsic rather than extraneous—in other words, the cognitive load is on the focus of the learning, rather than being peripheral to the intended learning. (For further information, see Bransford, Brown & Cocking 1999.)

The theory behind cognitive load is that working memory cannot process too many ideas simultaneously, so complexity can lead to inefficient or unproductive learning. Various commentators argue that cognitive load can be reduced by offering students worked examples. It is possible that narrow worked examples present mathematics as following set routines, whereas the scope of mathematics to be learned—even in school much less in life—is too broad to be reduced to routines.

When students are intended to merely replicate worked examples, this can prioritise fluency at the expense of understanding, problem solving and reasoning. Although some characteristics of worked examples are important—such as consideration of efficient strategies, clear set-out of responses, logical arguments and explaining thinking—these are more impactful when they occur *after* students have engaged with the task, rather than *before*. Further, the worked examples can be presented to the class by other students, rather than just the teacher, which emphasises the active role students have in creating new knowledge.

Ideally the following can be considered when discussing the suitability of tasks:

> the level of implied student choice, as student choice of focus, approach and difficulty contributes to motivation (see Middleton 1995)

> the potential for prompting communication, as communication can contribute to effective learning (see Wood 2005) and is more productive if there is more to discuss within the class than the correctness of the answer

> the degree of risk, as not all students respond well when they are uncertain on how to proceed or when the risk of failure is high (see Doyle 1986; Dweck 2000)

> the 'level' of potential student engagement. Fredericks, Blumfield and Paris (2004) describe engagement in terms of behavioural, emotional and cognitive responses. They argue that engagement is enhanced by tasks that are authentic. In other words, whether or not students can engage with tasks within their sense of self, they do not need to leave their personalities and dispositions at the classroom door in order to participate in mathematical activity. Thus mathematical tasks ideally provide opportunities for students' sense of ownership and personal meaning, as they foster collaboration, increase trust in student creativity, and provide fulfilment and empowerment.

One further consideration is the contribution that problem solving and reasoning make to learning. For example, when teachers structure their programs, it is common to focus first on building student understanding and fostering fluency, and then to pose problems and encourage students to reason as a final phase in the particular learning. However, it is possible to approach this the other way: to begin by posing tasks that are problems for the students and to encourage them to work on the problem to initiate learning. Student reasoning about the problem then helps them to understand the relevant concepts which, in turn, fosters mathematical fluency.

Choosing classroom tasks

To show how discussions might proceed, the following is an example of a classroom task suitable for Foundation level, but also relevant at most levels of primary school. There is also a task suitable for middle years students. The first task is from the 'Exploring mathematics sequences of connected cumulative challenging tasks' project, conducted by Monash University (Sullivan et al. 2019).

Tens frames

Make the number of counters on these frames the same—but without removing any counters from the left-hand frame. Do this as many different ways as you can.

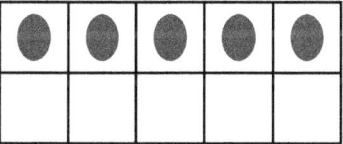
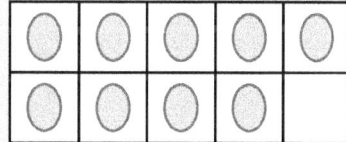

Readers are invited to find five distinct solutions. There are some obvious solutions, but there are also others that require some lateral thinking. The task can be readily modelled. The focus of this task is on more, less, equivalence, addition and subtraction.

If this task is done later in the year for Foundation-level students—and anytime for later years—students can be encouraged to record their responses numerically. For example, the solution found by moving two counters from the right-hand frame to the left, can be recorded as:

9 − 2 = 5 + 2

The possibilities of multiple answers gives students opportunities to compare the different types of equations, and to consider similarities and differences, for example:

9 = 5 + 4, 9 − 4 = 5, etc.

Teachers can encourage students to move beyond counting each counter each time, by reminding them that, 'The top row contains 5 counters, because we have counted it before'. A possible learning intention for the task is: 'We can make the collections equal and record our thinking with tens frames and number sentences.'

In discussing such a task, it is helpful for teachers to find a range of possible solutions and to discuss both the organisational and pedagogical issues associated with using such a task—especially in the early years. The explicit intention of describing this here is to emphasise that teacher commitment to such tasks is enhanced when school leaders are at the forefront of such discussions.

Another example of a classroom task suitable for students in Years 5-8 that focuses on equivalent fractions—depending on the level of sophistication expected—is outlined next.

Fractions of chocolate

Three friends shared this chocolate block, but they each got a different fraction of the whole and their fractions had different denominators.

What might have been the fractions?

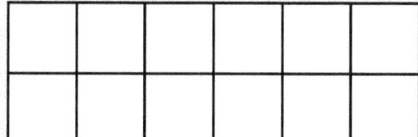

The first step for teachers when considering a task such as this—whether in a teacher professional learning session or a team-planning meeting—is to solve the task, preferably identifying all of the possibilities.

As an aside, readers are encouraged to find a systematic way to convince themselves that all possibilities have been found. There are four possible combinations, one of which is:

$$\frac{1}{12} + \frac{1}{6} + \frac{3}{4}$$

Then teachers can discuss the specific curriculum content descriptors potentially addressed through working on such a task, and ways in which the proficiencies are activated. In this case, students must first solve the problem, which includes:

› interpreting the problem statement

› finding a way to represent an answer

› checking that the answer actually solves the problem.

They can then explore ways of finding different possibilities. Such problem solving and reasoning helps to build understanding of the meaning of fractions, equivalent fractions and fraction addition. This, in turn, develops student fluency.

In the professional learning session or team-planning meeting, teachers can describe how this is similar to what they already do and how it is different, as well as discussing the opportunities for learning, the constraints they might anticipate and how the constraints might be overcome.

I emphasise that these tasks are presented as examples of the type of discussion that goes with choosing and discussing the potential of a task.

Summary and implications for professional learning

In summary, the main characteristic of a challenge is when students do not know how to solve the task, and work on that task before receiving any teacher instruction. Other features of appropriately challenging tasks are that they:

- build on what students already know
- take time—as the main difference between students is not some notional mathematical ability but the amount of time they need to engage with the ideas
- engage students, so that they are interested in the task and see value in persisting with it
- focus on important aspects of mathematics—as identified or implied in relevant curriculum documents
- use simple words, possibly drawing on relevant contexts or stories

> foster connections within mathematics and across domains of thinking

> foster choice and a sense of control by having more than one correct answer or more than one solution pathway.

Of course, not all tasks have all these characteristics, but tasks that do can productively be the focus of teacher professional learning. The ways that challenging tasks connect with the E2030 goals are elaborated in the conclusion of this book.

In the HITS document (Department of Education and Training 2017), the first of the strategies is 'setting goals':

> *Lessons have clear learning intentions with goals that clarify what success looks like. Lesson goals always explain what students need to understand, and what they must be able to do. This helps the teacher to plan learning activities, and helps students understand what is required.*

Even though Practice 2 in this book focuses on structuring lessons, the goals of mathematics classes are first determined by the tasks that teachers choose.

In terms of the work of Sullivan et al. (2016) discussed earlier, professional learning focusing on challenging tasks:

> addresses teachers' knowledge of mathematics and the nature of mathematical activity

> challenges teachers' beliefs, values and attitudes— especially those related to struggle

> allows consideration of constraints.

A particular barrier for teachers can be students' reluctance to take the time to engage with a task, as they can resent being expected to struggle with ideas. However, it seems that teachers can be encouraged to find ways to support students through such reluctance, rather than simplifying the tasks to avoid the struggle.

Teacher professional learning sessions could productively include:

> articulating the characteristics of tasks that are used commonly by the teachers

> listing the characteristics of tasks that might prompt student learning in new ways

> working through some examples of tasks that might be productive, and discussing ways that they align with common practice and ways they differ, especially focusing on which curriculum content descriptions they potentially address and which proficiencies the tasks can help students to experience

> considering available resources of tasks and creating opportunities for sharing tasks that have the desired characteristics

> discussing constraints teachers anticipate they might experience if posing such tasks with limited introduction, and how they might overcome those constraints.

Of course, the evidence of success of teachers' use of quality tasks is in student approaches to learning and student achievement. In the short term, the hope is for serious discussions in general conversations and teacher-planning meetings about the tasks and their potential, and the ways that they prompt learning.

PRACTICE 2

Improving student learning by addressing the structure of lessons

So far, my argument has been that there are benefits in engaging all students explicitly in exploring mathematical ideas, and that one approach to assisting teachers in engaging students is to focus on the quality of the tasks.

This chapter draws on the statement, attributed to John Hattie, that sets a goal of all students improving by 12 months each year, to propose that each one-hour lesson improves students' learning by 60 minutes. The second of the HITS (Department of Education and Training 2017) is 'structuring lessons'. This is summarised as follows:

> *A lesson structure maps teaching and learning that occurs in class. Sound lesson structures reinforce routines, scaffold*

learning via specific steps/activities. They optimise time on task and classroom climate by using smooth transitions. Planned sequencing of teaching and learning activities stimulates and maintains engagement by linking lesson and unit learning. (p. 8)

It is assumed that teacher professional learning and planning meetings that focus on the complexity of lessons and ways of improving those lessons will contribute to improved student learning.

Of course, there is no one structure for lessons and the overall classroom experience of students can be described as a 'balanced diet' of approaches.

Although this book argues that students benefit if teachers incorporate student-centred structured inquiry approaches into their repertoires more often, there are other common and productive lesson structures that achieve the goals listed earlier. For example, Russo and Hopkins (2017) argue that lessons that begin with explicit teacher guidance can still promote student 'puzzling', provided that:

> the tasks are sufficiently challenging

> the teacher is committed to maintaining the level of challenge as the task unfolds.

However, this explicit guidance does not imply that the teacher is explaining solution pathways; rather, they are eliciting prior knowledge and insights from the students as a starting point.

To elaborate on this point—and to emphasise not only the importance of structure in lessons but also that no one structure applies to all—the following section proposes four different templates that can be used to guide lesson planning and post-lesson reflection and critique. The templates are labelled:

> Active teaching

> Imagined representations

> Purposeful games and puzzles
> 'What if?'

A specific task is used to demonstrate each template, and the steps are explained. The intention is that teachers adapt the structure to other similar lessons, and that lesson structure becomes one of the focuses of an ongoing plan for teacher professional learning, as well as for informing discussions at level planning meetings.

An illustrative template for lessons focusing on understanding: Active teaching

It is productive for teachers to discuss ways in which tasks that foster conceptual understanding can be used as the focus of lessons.

The following template (adapted from Sullivan 2007) is similar to that described by Good, Grouws and Ebmeier (1983) as 'active teaching', which specifies the following activities, with the teacher having an active role at each stage:

> daily review of homework
> development—including addressing prerequisite skills, lively presentations, assessment of comprehension, and controlled practice
> seatwork
> homework assignment.

The template supports lessons in which teachers seek to develop comprehension of specific aspects of mathematics or to foster conceptual understanding of a procedure or technique. To illustrate the elements or phases of the template, suppose that teachers want their classes to learn the following:

Times 99

It is possible to multiply any number by 99 mentally by first multiplying by 100, then subtracting the number (based on Lovett & Clarke 1988).

Active teaching lesson template

The teacher poses some examples to check students have a grasp of the skills required, e.g. 600 − 6, and 1100 − 11.

The teacher poses some examples, e.g. 5 × 99, 8 × 99, and asks students to work out the answers. They ask some students to explain what they have done. The teacher then emphasises the method:

$$5 \times 99 = 5 \times (100 - 1) = 500 - 5 = 495$$

Further questions are posed, in sets of similar demand on students. The first set might be 6 × 99, the next set 11 × 99, and the next set 25 × 99, and then perhaps extending to 110 × 99.

Students' responses to set exercises are corrected. Some further examples are posed to check both students' accuracy and their capacity to explain the process they used, e.g. 4 × 99.

The specific example is suitable for upper primary or junior secondary students. This lesson template can be used to build understanding of ways of calculating, and to illustrate a purpose for the distributive law notation [**5 × 99 = 5 x (100 − 1)** etc.].

I emphasise that this is quite different from an approach where the teacher models a process to be followed, which the students then practise. Even though the lesson is led by the teacher, and proceeds in a lock-step approach, the focus is on student contribution to the learning and the lesson. There is opportunity early on for students to suggest their own methods, and later to extend the lesson to consideration of the general ways of writing such calculations. The experience is low in risk for students as the teacher guides the lesson; the engagement is through the teacher's energy, activity and explanations and, ideally, through students' desire for competence.

An illustrative template for lessons focusing on understanding: Purposeful games and puzzles

Purposeful games and puzzles (PGP; see Sullivan 2007) have the potential to form the basis of meaningful experiences that focus on the development of mathematical fluency.

However, it is worth noting that mathematics learning does not occur merely as an incidental component of engaging in the PGP. In this case, the intent of the template is to emphasise the mathematical purpose of the PGP, as well as to facilitate development of mathematical fluency in ways that have potential for future use.

The following is an example of a mathematical puzzle, adapted from a suggestion by Swan (n.d.). The puzzle involves a set of rectangular term (or number) cards and arrow operation cards, a subset of which could be the cards depicted in the following example.

Rectangles and arrows

[3a] [3a²b] →×b →÷b
             ←×ab ←÷ab

This example is suitable for junior secondary students. The puzzle is to choose the two operation cards that can be placed between the two term cards to represent the connection. In this case, the arrow card × **ab** connects **3a** to **3a²b**, and the other arrow card ÷ **ab** goes in the opposite direction. The point is that students have to look for the appropriate operation card to connect the terms and, by doing so, evaluate a range of possible operations simultaneously. It is also self-correcting, in that there are unique operations connecting the terms.

Note that the rectangular cards could be money amounts like $80 and $100, and the arrow cards could be, for example, 'up by 25%' 'down by 20%' and so on (of course, the actual set would be much larger than this). The operation can also be in decimals or fractions.

A generic lesson template for using such puzzles, and possible actions for this particular puzzle, follows. Of course, fluency is not the only likely learning outcome of such a lesson.

Purposeful games and puzzles lesson template

The teacher explains that there are two types of cards: rectangular cards with mathematical terms, and arrow cards with operations on them. The aim is to use the operation cards to connect the terms. The teacher then models the process using different but related cards.

After the students have worked on the task for a while, discuss as a class the processes for deciding which operation card is placed where, after which students can continue with the puzzle. Students can then be invited to describe how they made decisions about which operations cards to use.

The teacher monitors students' work as they arrange the cards. It is desirable to have both harder and easier sets of cards, for those who finish quickly, and for those find the puzzle too difficult. Some card sets might just involve numbers, or easier operations such as addition and subtraction. If necessary, it may be helpful to pose questions to assess learning such as $3a \times ? = 3a^2b$.

Variations can be introduced. Students can be asked to complete a set of practice exercises on operations with like terms, with the goal of emphasising fluency. Alternatively, students can be asked to create their own sets of term and operation cards.

The teacher can ask the students to suggest rules that can guide operations using algebraic terms, and to illustrate how the principles used in choosing the operation to connect $3a$ and $3a^2b$ can be extended to other operations.

The use of cards that can be manipulated reduces the risk of failure for students, which increases the chances of their participation as:

> students perform many calculations in a short period of time

> groups can be structured so that students learn from each other

> important mathematical processes are involved.

Note the importance of formalising the learning activated by the engagement with the activity or game.

An illustrative template for lessons focusing on problem solving: Imagined representations

The 'imagined representation' lesson template (Sullivan 2007) is suited to investigations that use a realistic, practical or pseudo-practical context seeking to foster strategic competence. The template is derived from activities suggested by Lovitt and Clarke (1988), such as 'Estimation with fractions', and 'How many people can stand in your classroom?'

The template provides a frame for those task-types discussed earlier that do not offer students something obvious to do, and supports teachers who are learning how to utilise tasks that are less structured than they are used to. There are many resources that propose contexts that draw on imagined representations, including:

> Maths 300 (available from https://maths300.com/)

> reSolve (available from https://www.resolve.edu.au/)

> Nrich (available from https://nrich.maths.org/).

The name 'Imagined representations' relates to the key element of problem solving—imagining possibilities. Here is an example of a lesson using Imagined representations that focuses on proportionality (and so is ideal for junior secondary students).

Statue of Liberty

The height of the Statue of Liberty is 46.05 metres. How long would you expect the statue's arm to be?

Imagined representation lesson template

The teacher asks students to work in groups to record an estimate of the length of the statue's arm. The estimation is intended to engender interest in the answer.

After discussion, compare groups' responses, which might include:

- using a photograph to compare the statue's height and the length of the arm
- measuring a sample of people to get a common ratio of height to arm length
- using ratios used by artists when representing people.

Groups of students are allocated to a particular solution strategy—preferably one they have suggested. Using whatever resources are required, they implement the particular strategy and prepare a report.

Students then report on their strategy, including their estimate of the length of the arm. The teachers can ask questions about the most accurate method of measurement, desired levels of accuracy, and the method students consider to be the most efficient.

Some similar ratio tasks can be posed that allow students to practise skills, or that prompt for transfer to alternate situations.

> **Imagined representation lesson template (continued)**
>
> The teacher emphasises the process for calculating ratios—which is the purpose of posing the task in the first place—as well as the steps necessary to ensure that data collected are accurate.

While it is difficult for the teacher to predict what will happen, this particular activity provides a context for:

- introduction of proportional reasoning and probability for application
- reinforcement of estimation and measurement of length.

This activity includes a metacognitive element, as it is not just contributing to students' awareness of the possibility of multiple appropriate strategies, but also their awareness of the usefulness of planning. It also:

- requires student choice of strategy—since they suggest which strategy to use
- has high potential for prompting communication— as students will be keen to explain what they found and how they found it
- poses medium risk—although students have some degree of choice, what they are required to do is ambiguous
- requires engagement through the potential for choice, and the interesting nature of the task.

This lesson template is applicable to any practical or realistic task that requires investigation or consideration of strategy by the students—especially where there is a need for students to imagine a representation.

An illustrative template for lessons focusing on reasoning: The 'What if?' template

The 'What if?' template is useful for open-ended and mathematically focused investigative tasks. Opening up tasks can:

> engage students in productive exploration (Christiansen & Walther 1986)

> enhance motivation by increasing students' sense of control (Middleton 1995)

> encourage pupils to investigate, make decisions, generalise, seek patterns and connections, communicate, discuss, and identify alternatives (Sullivan 1999).

The following is an example of a task suitable for this template. It is appropriate for upper primary students, but also useful at junior secondary level.

Length of the string

You have a box that needs 1 m of string to tie it up like this. What might be the dimensions of the box?
　　Note: Assume you need 30 cm to make the bow.

Even though students are constrained by the length of the string, there are still many possible solutions—and many ways of representing those solutions. The task connects the 2D representation of a box to a real or imagined box, and encourages students to think in three dimensions rather than just applying a rule with little understanding.

'What if?' lesson template

The teacher might begin by posing the problem, and clarifying terms and meanings. Students might be invited to record their answers systematically. The teacher might pose a preliminary problem, such as: 'How might you calculate the length of the string on this box without untying it?'

The teacher monitors students' work. Some students will have difficulty answering the question, so the teacher could prepare some boxes and loose string for those students who need to tie up a box, or a box covered in a streamer that could be cut into sections.

For students who produce one or more correct responses, the teacher might ask them to find as many answers as possible—for example, the smallest box, the nicest box, etc.

The teacher could invite some students with simple strategies to demonstrate their strategies to the class. Next, the teacher might choose a student who had produced an organised response to summarise their answers to the whole group. Students who have different responses can also be invited to contribute their answers.

Finally, the teacher can summarise the successful strategies and the collective responses. This is the key part of the lesson for drawing out the patterns, commonalities and generalisations.

A lesson in using the What if? template focuses on adaptive reasoning—although there are also possibilities for fostering conceptual understanding and strategic competence, as:

> there is student choice in the strategy to be used—as students choose the degree of difficulty and the mode of representation

> it is an appropriate task for prompting communication—as students have the products of their own explorations to contribute

> it is low-risk—as students have choice in strategies and the level at which they work

> it is engaging—through student choice of strategy, and the challenge of the task.

Some elements common to each template

There are some aspects of teaching that apply across each template. Drawing on Sullivan et al. (2016), it is argued that all lessons can include the following characteristics:

> Tasks are posed without telling students how to solve them, even though in many lessons review of prior learning and consideration of unfamiliar aspects is important, such as introduction of new terminology.

> Students are allowed time to engage with tasks initially by themselves, and perhaps later in small groups.

> Actions are taken by the teacher to differentiate tasks for students who might require additional support and those who finish quickly (see Practice 4).

> Student responses to the tasks are observed and selected by the teacher during the lesson to foster classroom dialogue between students, emphasising students' explorations and mathematical thinking.

Note the connection to HITS 4 (Department of Education and Training 2017), 'worked examples':

A worked example demonstrates the steps required to complete a task or solve a problem. By scaffolding the learning, worked examples support skill acquisition and reduce a learner's cognitive load. The teacher presents a worked example and explains each step. Later, students can use worked examples during independent practice, and to review and embed new knowledge.

In this proposed lesson structure, the worked examples *follow* students engaging with the problem, rather than *preceding it*. Note also that the worked examples might be those created by students and chosen by the teacher, or created by the teacher.

Also applicable to each template are the five practices described by Smith and Stein (2011):

> Anticipating expected student responses—this happens before the lesson and involves the teacher working through the task and imagining how students might respond.

> Monitoring student work—which connects to the formative assessment potential of such learning.

> Selecting examples for students to present or discuss—these are chosen to foster discussion, not just to show the best ways of responding.

> Sequencing the presentation of those responses—with the intent that the key mathematical ideas will emerge progressively.

> Connecting student responses to the mathematical purpose of the task students are working on.

Note the connection to HITS 3 (Department of Education and Training 2017), 'explicit teaching':

> *When teachers adopt explicit teaching practices they clearly show students what to do and how to do it. The teacher decides on learning intentions and success criteria, makes them transparent to students, and demonstrates them by modelling. The teacher checks for understanding, and at the end of each lesson revisits what was covered and ties it all together (Hattie 2009).*

Two further practices are also relevant for each of the templates: the notion of encouraging students to listen to others; and using efficient ways to allow students to present their completed work to the class.

Each of the four templates can also follow the common three-part lesson—with the important qualification that this triad can occur more than once in a single lesson:

> launch—without telling the students what to do

> explore—having students engage with the problem by themselves or in small groups

> summarise—eliciting students' insights and solutions.

It is also relevant to add a fourth step:

> review–the teacher summarises the key ideas already articulated and introduces further syntheses not already identified.

An additional component relevant to each template is that it is common for teachers to allocate about 10 minutes for number talks, fluency games and activities at the start of lessons. Rather than just random practice, there are distinct advantages when fluency activities prepare students specifically for the upcoming learning experiences. This has a double effect, as:

> the fluency helps to activate knowledge required for the upcoming task

> the task, in turn, can reinforce the initial development of fluency.

Some elements of the 'Fractions of chocolate' lesson

Following is an illustration of how these generic elements apply to the 'Fractions of chocolate' task described earlier (see p. 25), and some key actions to show how the lesson might develop.

FLUENCY FOR THE LESSON

Just like with whole numbers, saying fractions sequences in order—especially when attending to equivalences in naming, for example, $\frac{1}{2}$ is the same as $\frac{2}{4}$. These sequences can help students solve problems such as 'Fractions of chocolate'. Following is an example of a counting activity that is engaging, but without being competitive.

Counting activity

In small groups, students stand in a circle and say the next number in a sequence, forwards or backwards, from a given starting point. Each student uses their hand to indicate who says the next number in the sequence (to the left or to the right).

In getting ready for such lessons, at different times the counting can be in steps of halves, quarters, eighths, thirds, sixths, and so on. For example, the count in eighths would be one-eighth, one-quarter, three-eighths, one-half, five-eighths, three-quarters, seven-eighths, one, one and one-eighth, and so on.

It is surprising how quickly upper primary students learn to do this when saying number sequences that have both a physical and an intellectual demand.

LAUNCHING THE PROBLEM

The next step is the introduction. In each of the templates, the intention is to allow students time to work on the problem without having been told what to do. But it is also helpful to avoid time-consuming confusion, and to anticipate issues that are not germane to the problem.

For example, assuming that interpreting the problem— especially the constraint that the answers are different—might present unnecessary initial confusion, it would be possible to invite, say, 11 students to stand and get into three groups with each grouping having a different number of students. They can be told not to talk or push, but to look at what others are doing and make decisions. Such an activity can also allow discussion of the possibility of multiple answers.

While this may be a matter of taste, I prefer that students above Year 2 read the problem for themselves, inviting questions about words or ideas that are not clear. This is for two reasons. First, reading the question at a self-determined pace increases the chances that students read the key aspects. Second, learning to read problems is a key skill that is useful in many domains. It is helpful to revise prerequisite and new language—including attention to pronunciation issues, such as saying 'one-eighth' differently from 'one eight'.

Depending on student familiarity with this lesson approach, you could revise class rules, especially if you prefer that students work individually first, with working in pairs or groups taking place subsequently.

EXPLORING

It is common to see that once the teacher has set students to work in the classroom, a number of students raise their hands seeking help. Such students need to learn to first engage with the problem—even if they do not know how to proceed. Rather than assisting students, the role of the teacher is to move around the room, observing, interacting with students and making decisions about what should happen next.

Of course, part of this role is encouraging students to persist. There are a number of actions that can be part of more or less every class. For example, it is common for teachers to use the rule of '4 before me', by creating rules that students are required to follow before they can ask for help, such as the following:

> 'Reread the question.'
> 'Start again a different way.'
> 'Ask a friend.'
> 'Look back through your book.'

Some teachers tell students that they have a 'Zone of confusion' in the class, and it is expected that they will go into the zone more or less in every lesson. Another strategy is to have a standard set of workbooks, such as:

- writing what is known at the top of the page
- using the middle of the page for rough work
- using the bottom of the page for neat answers.

Further, while the students are exploring, the teacher can anticipate what might happen at the review phase, and select and sequence some student work that can be productively discussed with the class.

The teacher might also plan ways of differentiating the task for individual students. This is discussed in detail in Practice 4.

REVIEWING STUDENT WORK AND SUMMARISING THE KEY MATHEMATICAL IDEAS

After most students have made progress on the task, there can be a class discussion of what students have found. The students whose work has been selected can outline the strategies they have used. It is useful to have a way of projecting student work. There are various technological solutions for this.

The role of the teacher at this stage is:

- to support students in explaining their work
- to encourage other students to pay attention—for example: 'What do you think Emily did?', 'In what ways was what you did similar to (or different from) Emily?' and so on
- to emphasise key mathematical ideas that have arisen.

The teacher can also restate and synthesise the ideas that have been presented, as well as giving an indication of what happens next.

Summary and implications for professional learning

Planning real or imaginary lessons is seen by teachers as practical and authentic, a worthwhile way to spend time, and it helps to provide a direct connection between theoretical considerations and practical imperatives.

The argument here is that lessons that start with the teacher telling students what to do have no long-term benefits, nor do lessons in which students work in an unstructured way on vague inquiries. Whatever the content focus, lessons are best when they are student-centred—but with a deliberate structure. In fact, the skill of imagining how a lesson might develop can be a key focus of professional learning.

The suggestions in Practice 2 incorporate the characteristics of tasks described in Practice 1. Some of the specific issues on which professional learning and teacher-planning sessions might focus are:

> ways of introducing tasks and lessons that preserve the challenge, and engage students in thinking about mathematics for themselves

> strategies for 'holding back', and giving students time to think and to struggle

> ways of using strategies and solutions suggested by students as key parts of the learning, and the assessment possibilities of doing this

> the different types of lesson structures that constitute a 'balanced diet' of approaches and ways of learning

> ways the lesson structure can inform teacher reflection and collaborative lesson observations

> the importance of teacher flexibility and 'thinking on your feet'.

Progress in planning lessons will be mainly evident in the documentation, but also in the quality of the language teachers use when describing and reflecting on lessons.

PRACTICE 3

The development and use of learning sequences to inform high-quality classroom learning

As has been argued earlier, choosing tasks that are potentially mathematically and pedagogically rich is most likely to prompt deep learning. Lessons can then be structured around those tasks. So far, the cognition of the students has been activated—and now the learning can be consolidated. This process for consolidating learning connects to considering sequences or trajectories of learning over a longer timeframe than a single lesson.

The planning and documentation of lessons can be an important component of school-based strategies for improving learning. This is especially important, as many commonly available resources present an idea as a 'one-off', and do not anticipate the need for teachers to consolidate learning, as is described in this practice.

Sequences of learning are created when teachers pose further tasks that are in some ways similar and in some ways different from the initial task. There are two ways of doing this, with differing results. If the teacher:

> keeps the context the same but varies the concept in subsequent tasks; this contributes to building understanding and fostering connections within mathematical domains

> keeps the concept the same but varies the context; this prompts transfer and stimulates connections across domains.

Variation theory informs the design of such sequences. Kullberg, Runesson and Mårtensson (2013), for example, argue:

> *In order to understand or see a phenomenon or a situation in a particular way one must discern all the critical aspects of the object in question simultaneously. Since an aspect is* noticeable only if it varies against a background in invariance *[emphasis in original], the experience of variation is a necessary condition for learning something in a specific way. (p. 611)*

In a similar way, Dreyfus and Tsamir (2004) describe consolidation through task variation:

> *A novel mental structure that has not been consolidated is likely to be fragile. It may be at the learner's disposal only in a specific context, under certain circumstances, in certain representations and when dealing with a certain type of problems.*

> *Consolidation allows a student to make fluent and confident use of the abstract notion in varied situations. (p. 273)*

Connected to the notion of consolidation and the creation of sequences is what Simon (1995) describes as a hypothetical learning trajectory that:

> *provides the teacher with a rationale for choosing a particular instructional design; thus, I (as a teacher) make my design decisions based on my best guess of how learning might proceed. This can be seen in the thinking and planning that preceded my instructional interventions ... as well as the spontaneous decisions that I make in response to students' thinking. (pp. 135–6)*

The issue of spontaneous decision-making is important, especially in choosing what students might do next. Few lessons go entirely as planned, so it is helpful for teachers to have principles that guide their interactive decision-making.

Simon's (1995) hypothetical learning trajectory is made up of three components:

> the learning goal that determines the desired direction of teaching and learning

> the sequence of experiences to be undertaken by the teacher and students

> a hypothetical cognitive process, 'a prediction of how the students' thinking and understanding will evolve in the context of the learning activities' (p. 136).

The learning goal can be related to the documented curriculum, or it can be an outcome of particular concepts found to be difficult for some students to learn.

The notion of sequences of learning applies regardless of the form of the lesson, especially those described in Practice 2. These predictions of the development of understanding are not related to students listening to a hierarchy of explanations, but to them engaging with a succession of problem-like tasks.

In planning (and teaching), the role of the teacher is to identify when concepts have been learned, so that they can be used flexibly. In other words, learning occurs as a product of students working on sequences of tasks purposefully selected by the teacher, and by them communicating with the teacher and their peers about their answers and the strategies they used to arrive at the answers.

This notion is described in the HITS document (Department of Education and Training 2017) as 'multiple exposures'. Specifically:

> *Multiple exposures provide students with multiple opportunities to encounter, engage with, and elaborate on new knowledge and skills. Research demonstrates deep learning develops over time via multiple, spaced interactions with new knowledge and concepts. This may require spacing practice over several days, and using different activities to vary the interactions learners have with new knowledge. (p. 9)*

Some of the advantages of specifically planned sequences of learning for students and teachers are as follows:

1. Sequences can help students see the 'bigger picture'. One of the disadvantages of conventional approaches to mathematics and numeracy is that mathematics can seem to be broken into sets of micro skills, rather than contributing to a coherent whole. Sequences may help students see connections by making the 'big ideas' and progression of learning more obvious to them.

Sequencing connects to the HITS-termed 'metacognition', which is intended to:

teach students to think about their own thinking. When students become aware of the learning process, they gain control over their learning. Metacognition extends to self-regulation, or managing one's own motivation toward learning. Metacognitive activities can include planning how to approach learning tasks, evaluating progress, and monitoring comprehension.
(Department of Education and Training 2017)

2. Concepts are learned as much by what they are not, as by what they are. For example, the attribute of height is different from that of volume; when do three lines make a triangle, and when they do not, etc. Carefully varied tasks within sequences can emphasise what the central ideas are—and what they are not—which allows students to discern the essence of concepts.

3. Sequences of challenging tasks can prompt 'light-bulb' moments—but there are no light bulbs if students are told what to do. Students can benefit from working on tasks that are challenging, and progressively see meaning by experiencing connected tasks, with success also developing progressively, especially where the insights or 'aha' moments are the result of their own thinking.

4. Sequences can reduce the sense of risk that some students experience. Many teachers report that some students do not embrace challenges because they are afraid of failing. One of the goals of learning sequences is for students to see that—even if they cannot do the current task—there is a similar task coming, and they can work out how to do subsequent tasks by engaging in the current task and listening to the peers and the teacher, even if they are not yet successful.

Following are some examples of consolidating tasks, by making a sequence to follow up the 'Length of the string' task in Practice 2. It is assumed that the original task would have activated students' thinking about:

> dimensions

> imagining the box and string from the diagram

> different possible answers with one length of string

> how if one dimension varies, then so will the others.

There is also an element about unit conversions.
An example of a possible sequence of tasks follows.

2.5 m of string

You have a box that needs 2.5 m of string to tie it up like this. What might be the dimensions of the box?
Note: Assume you need 50 cm to make the bow.

Give at least three possible answers.

This is essentially the same task as presented in 'What if?' in Practice 2, but using different numbers. The intent is that students learn by working on the first task. With this task it is hoped, for example, that students would be exposed to experience related to:

> the dimensions of 3D objects
> the role of diagrams and visualisation
> the need for working and thinking systematically
> the potential for generalising.

Even if students are not successful, they will have heard the contributions from other students and the teacher, and will be able to attempt this task more readily than the first. If more tasks like this are needed, the teacher can pose them by varying the dimensions given.

How much string?

You have a box like this that is 50 cm wide, 20 cm high and 30 cm deep. The bow takes 30 cm. How much string do you need?

Work this out in two different ways.

In this example, the context is the same, but this time the dimensions are given—which means that there is only one correct answer. Finding a solution in two different ways is intended to prompt students to see the similarities and differences in their solution strategies.

Using two methods can perhaps encourage students to check their answers for accuracy using a different method. If needed, more examples like this can be created using different numbers.

Length of the frame

I want to make the frame of a box like this using sticks, although not all of the sticks are shown.

If the frame is to be 1 m high, 2 m deep and 3.5 m wide, what is the total length of the sticks needed to make the frame?

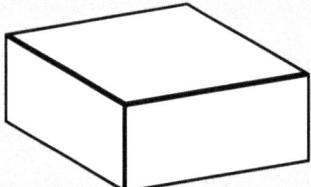

Work this out in two different ways.

Even though the context is similar, now there is no bow involved. The hope is that students not only see that they can apply their learned strategies to this task, but also that what they now know can be applied in a variety of situations involving rectangular prisms—and perhaps other prisms as well.

The intention is that teachers continue to propose variations on the original task so that as many students as possible consolidate their learning. Student work is assessed progressively. The guiding principle is that it is better to consolidate this learning now, than to rush to a different topic.

Summary and implications for professional learning

Of course, all teacher planning focuses on sequences of learning. Unfortunately, many teachers see the scope of the curriculum as a priority and emphasise broad coverage over the sequence of learning.

Essentially, students learn better when fewer topics are done well, rather than when more topics are done quickly. Part of the reason for this is that some students develop so little over time that much of their learning is superficial. The argument is that designed sequences of learning, or multiple exposures, can contribute to improved and robust learning, and to fostering metacognition.

In every collaborative team-planning session, the focus can be on:

> identifying the main focus of learning and how teachers can assess progress to identify when students have learned the key ideas or when more experience is needed

> ways of consolidating learning through either:

- keeping the context the same, but varying the nature of the question—which might just mean changing the numbers
- keeping the concept the same, but varying the context.

The attention to planning and teaching sequences of experiences intended to consolidate learning will be evident in the documentation of learning plans, discussed in Practice 6.

PRACTICE 4

Teacher professional learning that focuses on grouping practices

So far, the discussion on aspects of planning and teaching has assumed that students at a particular level have the same mathematical experience and readiness. But this is not the case. Perhaps the most significant challenge for school leaders and teachers in planning and teaching mathematics is to ensure that all students experience the full curriculum for as long as possible.

Teachers often report that their major difficulty is dealing with differences in prior experience, achievement, motivation, persistence and aspiration, as well as the extent to which students see schooling—especially in mathematics—as creating future opportunities. The discussion of Practice 4:

> › outlines the community expectation—which aligns with the E2030 aspirations—that schools create opportunities for all students

> challenges simplistic solutions to grouping for mathematics teaching

> outlines some approaches to engaging all students— especially within whole-class mixed-achievement teaching

> outlines the rationale for a particular approach to intervention.

Each of these aspects is relevant for school leaders who become involved in decisions about grouping practices, and who may even need to adjudicate between competing perspectives. The following discussion is based on Sullivan (2015).

Fundamental to system, school and classroom decisions about maximising opportunity is the potential of education to create opportunities that students might not otherwise have. The commitment of government through its various agencies is quite clear, as evidenced in the overarching 'Shape Paper' (ACARA 2012) that established the principles for the Australian Curriculum (AC):

> *All Australian governments have committed to the goals of the Melbourne Declaration, which are that Australian schooling promotes equity and excellence; and that all young Australians become successful learners, confident and creative individuals, and active and informed citizens. (p. 5)*

The 'Shape Paper' goes further, arguing that schooling and the curriculum should ensure that young people 'have a sense of self-worth, self-awareness and personal identity that enables them to manage their emotional, mental, spiritual and physical wellbeing' (p. 8).

This, in turn, is intended to prepare students for further study, careers and life as productive citizens. The 'Shape Paper' (2012) even discusses the 'entitlement' each student has 'to knowledge, skills and understandings that provide a foundation for successful and lifelong learning and participation in the Australian community' (p. 10). The paper also makes the explicit assumption that:

> *each student can learn and the needs of every student are important. It enables high expectations to be set for each student as teachers account for the current levels of learning of individual students and the different rates at which students develop. (p. 10)*

Similar sentiments are expressed in the principles for mathematics (ACARA 2009):

> *Building on the draft National Declaration on Educational Goals for Young Australians, a fundamental aim of the mathematics curriculum is to educate students to be active, thinking citizens, interpreting the world mathematically, and using mathematics to help form their predictions and decisions about personal and financial priorities. Mathematics also enables and enriches study and practice in many other disciplines. (p. 5)*

The 2009 ACARA document also argues that the opportunities created by schooling should be available for all students, and that those opportunities should be preserved for as long as possible. In particular, mathematics is often used as a filter, and it is possible that some students are excluded from further study and career options by capricious planning decisions.

In other words, the documents—which can be assumed to represent community aspirations—argue that all students have an entitlement to a curriculum that maximises their opportunities, and prepares them for a life in which creativity, imagination and an orientation towards life-long learning are emphasised more than correct answers, compliant attitudes and acceptance of a designated place in a hierarchical social order. The assumption is that schools and classrooms should be structured to facilitate achievement of the curriculum goals for *all* students.

In the HITS (Department of Education and Training 2017) document, this approach is described as 'differentiated teaching', which refers to the:

> *methods teachers use to extend the knowledge and skills of every student in every class, regardless of their starting point. The objective is to lift the performance of all students, including those who are falling behind and those ahead of year level expectations. To ensure all students master objectives, effective teachers plan lessons that incorporate adjustments for content, process, and product.*

A key challenge for schools is to find ways to address the needs of all students. But a critical consideration is that within each grouping of students there is widespread diversity.

In exploring this issue, Thompson, De Bortoli, Nicholas, Hillman and Buckley (2010) compared the reading levels of Australian-born students, first-generation students, and foreign-born students. First-generation students had a slight advantage—but the real issue is that the diversity of achievement in each of the three groups of students was more or less identical, as there were similar proportions of students from each group at each of the achievement levels defined by PISA.

There is a similar diversity of achievement among low-SES group students, First Nations students and rural students, with some students in each of these groupings achieving at the top international levels. The challenge for schools is to ensure that some students are not given a restricted curriculum based solely on some group characteristic, but for schools to find ways to address the diversity of readiness whatever the student population.

In other words, even though there is a long tail in the achievement of Australian students, with particular subgroups over-represented in the tail, there are also students even within the subgroups achieving at the best international levels. These factors make the task of structuring schools and classrooms to maximise opportunity challenging.

Accommodating the diversity of readiness in school and classroom grouping structures

It is not a simple task to address the diversity of readiness and the challenges that teachers face. The focus in this practice is on ways that schools respond to these pressures and, in particular, on the decisions that are made about the ways that students are grouped.

Such grouping decisions are often made based on the preferences of teachers, and can be informed by their views on who can learn, and by their concerns for particular categories of students that they feel might be disadvantaged by certain school and class groupings. These issues are especially acute in mathematics classes, where stratification of groups is most prevalent. It is argued here that schools and teachers need to make informed choices about types of student grouping, and to be aware of—and thus avoid—the threats in particular types of grouping.

Schools and teachers address such differences in various ways. After a curriculum project, Sullivan, Clarke and Clarke (2013) found that around one-third of teachers reported that they grouped students by achievement with each group working on related tasks. Just under one-third chose the option: 'Whole class teaching, with everyone working on the same tasks with you assisting individual students, with some students completing more than others'. Just under one-third chose the option: 'Whole class teaching, working on similar tasks, differentiated for students who experience difficulty in starting and/or who are ready for more challenge'.

Interestingly, very few teachers chose the option: 'Students grouped by achievement with each group working on unrelated tasks', or 'Whole class teaching, with everyone working on similar tasks and you choose a like achievement group with whom you work for most of the lesson'.

One common form of stratification is when students are assessed in mathematics and then grouped according to the results of that assessment. Although different terms are used, this is called *streaming* when the grouping is just for mathematics. There are also schools that select one or more high-achieving groups for all subjects, but otherwise have the rest of the groups grouped heterogeneously—which is commonly described as *tracking*.

Some of the threats that have been identified with heterogeneous groupings are that:

> teachers set expectations and starting points based on low-achieving students and, as a result, other students are under-extended and less satisfied with their learning environment

> teachers assume low-achieving students cannot cope and over direct the learning of the whole class, which encourages students to have a fixed mindset (Dweck 2000) and a passive approach to learning

> there is negative peer pressure on hard-working students, which is very real. For example, Sullivan, Tobias and McDonough (2006) have found that the classroom culture exerts a more powerful negative influence on students than their individual aspirations

> teachers can ignore the diversity of readiness and instead treat everyone as the same—possibly by giving routine tasks that all students can and are willing to do (see Doyle 1986)

> teachers teach different content to different groups—which not only increases the teachers' workload but destroys any sense of a classroom community

> low-achieving students 'performance avoid' (Elliot 1999) by misbehaving, being a group-work passenger, or by pretending to work while not actually doing anything.

Clearly, if heterogeneous groups are to maximise the learning of all students, then substantial actions must be taken by teachers and schools to anticipate and address such threats.

On the other hand, homogeneous groupings can have the effect of restricting student opportunities if:

> teachers teach different content to different groups—which not only narrows the options of some students but closes them off too early

> there is limited or no movement between groups, which appears to be the most common situation. If there is no chance of 'promotion', students are unlikely to try hard. Students can also develop a group affiliation and artificially underperform to avoid being moved

> steps are not taken to avoid development of poor self-concept by some members of the upper streams. Marsh, Craven and McInerney (2005) describe this as the 'big fish little pond' effect, in which a substantial minority of students in such groups develop a low self-concept—and subsequent limited interest in the subject—because they feel that their classmates are more able than they are.

However, there are significant barriers to overcoming the negative effects of homogeneous grouping. It is very difficult to ensure that students in all groups have the same opportunities if the curriculum is stratified and only a limited subset of the curriculum is offered to some groups. This can be exacerbated if teachers feel that fluency with routines precedes other learning, and so emphasise skills to the detriment of other aspects of mathematics, such as communication, meaning and relevance. Indeed, just placing students in low streams tells them that their teachers think they cannot learn. A further risk is that the 'homogeneous' grouping of students tells teachers that the students are of like achievement—and they are then treated as though they are all the same.

Further, even class groups designed to maximise homogeneity are diverse in their readiness. The explanation for this is that even though students are grouped by their achievement, the intent of streaming is to group students by their *ability*, which cannot be measured directly. Because there are high-ability students who may achieve low scores on a particular assessment for a variety of reasons—and some low-ability students who score well, perhaps due to their effort or after-school tuition—even like achievement groups will have a range of abilities. In other words, if students are grouped according to their achievement, there will still be a diversity of readiness to learn mathematics—and all teachers need to plan to address this diversity.

More conclusively, in a major meta-analysis, Hattie (2009) argues that stratification, streaming, tracking and setting has 'minimal effect on learning outcomes and profound negative equity effects' (p. 90). He explains that low-stream classes are 'deadening, non-educational environments' (p. 90) that fail 'to foster the outcomes schools value' but are focused on 'remediation through dull, repetitious seatwork'. Yet Hattie also proposes that 'it seems that the quality of teaching and the nature of students' interactions are the key issues, rather than the compositional structure of the classes' (p. 91).

Brophy (1983) suggests that being aware of the potential impact of self-fulfilling prophesies on particular groupings can minimise negative effects. For example, teachers in both heterogeneous and homogeneous groups can avoid the impact of their presumptions about individual students' potential by consciously treating all students similarly.

In other words, streaming students for mathematics classes poses a threat to equity and opportunity, but the ways classes are taught is just as important as the method of grouping.

Ways of dealing with difference while maintaining a coherent and inclusive class community

So far, readers might be thinking, 'This advice is unrealistic'. Central to the practices being advocated in this book is an effective and efficient way of ensuring that all students in the class proceed at an optimal pace. Some teachers are concerned at the risks associated with posing challenges, out of fear that some students might find the struggle unproductive. And the importance of extending students who are ready is just as critical for consideration in planning and teaching.

The following section outlines some strategies that can be part of everyday planning and teaching. One strategy is to choose tasks that are flexible enough that students can respond in different ways to the same task. For example, referring again to the 'Length of the string' task, the teacher might be satisfied if some students can find one solution, while others find many solutions, with some students even finding the general way to report all the possibilities.

Such tasks can be described as 'low floor and high ceiling'. The term 'floor' refers to a single response that might represent an achievement for some students. In the case of the 'Length of the string' task (see p. 41), students who find a single solution (such as length = 5 cm, width = 10 cm, height = 10 cm) would be considered to have reached the floor. 'Ceiling' refers to the broader potential of the task.

For example, a student who created an equation such as

4H + 2L + 2W = 70

is seeking to generalise the solution and would be approaching an expected ceiling. Tasks that have more than one possible answer are ideal for this. If students respond with one correct solution, they feel they have achieved, but other students can give more sophisticated responses. Both types of students are more likely to be engaged because they chose not only their approach, but also the sophistication of their response. In other words, the task itself allows ready differentiation.

As part of planning, teachers can also prepare specific prompts for students who might have difficulty—called 'enabling prompts'. Such prompts to students are a variation on the main task, and are created by:

> posing a change to the representation

> reducing the size of the numbers involved, or

> reducing the number of steps.

The intention with an enabling prompt is that once the prompt is completed, the students return to the original challenge.

In the case of the 'Length of the string' task, enabling prompts might be:

> to have some boxes available that are tied like the diagram, for students to look at

> to ask students to suggest how they might work out the length of the string needed to tie up the box, but without untying the string

> to have an adaptation of the original task prepared to hand out to students who still have not progressed, as outlined next.

60 cm of string

If I need 60 cm of string to tie up a box like this, what might be the length and height of the box?

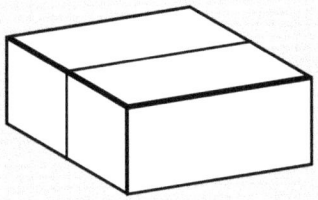

Note that this is a similar task with some of the complexity removed, which makes it more accessible, and provides a scaffold to the original task. Some teachers might respond by suggesting that this task be posed first, yet there are substantial advantages from starting with the more complex task, as is explained in the discussion of Practice 1.

Using such enabling prompts consistently reassure students that assistance is available if needed, and also helps them to learn self-help strategies through the modelling involved in this process.

Students who finish quickly can be extended if teachers have prepared prompts to extend the thinking of students who have solved the initial task. Such extending prompts are best when they prompt abstraction and generalisation of the ideas represented by the initial challenge. In the case of the 'Length of the string' task some options include:

> making the representation more complex, perhaps by posing a further question without a diagram

> changing the numbers to make it more complex, perhaps using fractions or decimals

> increasing the number of steps, by making the placement of the string more complex

> prompting students to generalise—for example, 'Find a way to describe all of the possible answers to the question'

> encouraging students to create their own question like the original task posed.

Of the earlier tasks, 'Fractions of chocolate' (p. 25), 'Rectangles and arrows' (p. 36) and the 'Statue of Liberty' (p. 39) can also be considered to be low floor and high ceiling, as students can respond to the same task at different levels of sophistication—and even discuss their different responses with each other. The concept of enabling and extending prompts applies to each of the tasks and lessons described earlier, including 'Times 99' (p. 34).

A promising approach to intervention

Even with specific actions by teachers to differentiate learning opportunities, there can still be students who experience difficulty in learning, especially at upper primary and junior secondary levels. This section describes a program for re-engaging disengaged students that is different from common 'catch them up' approaches. The intervention 'Getting Ready in Numeracy' (GRIN) aims to prepare students for mathematics classroom experiences they will have subsequent to the tutoring.

There are three separate but critical components that are addressed in the professional learning associated with GRIN:

> Teachers plan sequences of lessons with specific goals that address the diversity of students' prior mathematical knowledge.

> Teachers communicate the goals of the upcoming lessons to the tutor.

> Tutors plan intervention sessions that include three elements aimed at getting students ready for subsequent learning:

- targeted fluency practice
- language development
- developing familiarity with key prerequisite concepts.

For example, if the teacher was planning an introduction to the theorem of Pythagoras, and has communicated that intention to the tutor, the tutor might:

> plan to revisit squares and square roots

> explore what students know about the hypotenuse

> revise equations with unknowns and properties of right-angled triangles.

These are prerequisite to the learning of the theorem, and would not detract from the lesson itself. The tutoring gets students ready for the subsequent learning. There is a double advantage in that students not only learn prerequisite concepts in the tutoring session, but also in the mathematics class.

GRIN is informed by two complementary strands of research: the first based on views of cognition; and the second associated with student disposition and the social context of the classroom.

Part of the rationale for this intervention is derived from cognitive load theory. As described by Bransford, Brown and Cocking (1999), cognitive load theory suggests that information is processed in working memory and then stored in long-term memory. Ideally, information stored in long-term memory is efficiently chunked, so that it can be readily retrieved. The initial processing of information and preparation for this chunking happens in working memory, which is of limited capacity.

In classrooms, students *attend* to stimuli around them and then *select* information for processing. Students who are not familiar with prerequisite concepts and language have difficulty in selecting appropriately, and consequently the instruction, the task, the language—and even what other students are saying and doing—overloads their working memory. A particular explanation of ways that cognitive load informs the design of tasks—and student responses to learning experiences—is described by Russo (2015). The intervention process seeks to focus students' attention onto the key concepts, and to allow them to select information appropriately.

The other rationale for the program is social or affective. Teachers commonly encounter students who have come to believe that they cannot learn mathematics, which limits their willingness to engage with learning experiences. For example, Martin and Marsh (2006) have found that self-concept is a key determinant of learning outcomes for all students, and that negative self-concept is especially detrimental for low-achieving students. Dweck (2000) proposes that finding ways to support low-achieving students is as much connected to their orientation to learning as it is to the level of their knowledge.

Dweck categorises students' orientation to learning in terms of whether they hold either mastery goals or performance goals. Dweck argues that students with mastery goals seek to understand the content, and evaluate their success by whether they feel they can use and transfer their knowledge. In contrast, students with performance goals are, at best, interested in whether they can perform assigned tasks correctly. Dweck connects performance goals to a fixed view of intelligence, where students believe that the intelligence that they have is what they were born with and which cannot be changed. Students with mastery goals see intelligence as incremental, and feel they can change their intelligence or achievement depending on factors over which they have some control.

More critical for students from middle primary levels upwards is what Elliot (1999) describes as 'performance avoidance'. In this, some students choose not to engage in a task or experience at all, rather than attempting the task and failing (see also Desforges & Cockburn 1987). The underlying assumption is that if the risk of failure is reduced through increased familiarity with the focus content and associated processes, then students who would otherwise be disinclined to participate may join in with others in attempting the tasks set.

Summary and implications for professional learning

In summary, this practice focuses on ways of offering a full curriculum to all students and taking action to ensure that they engage in the learning opportunities. The risks and opportunities in both homogeneous and heterogeneous groups have been described. In particular, strategies for supporting the learning of all students have been outlined.

It is proposed that teacher professional learning, and processes within planning teams, focus on the identification or creation of 'low floor and high ceiling' tasks, and prompts that can both support the learning of those experiencing difficulty and those who are ready for some extension. Note that the processes of consolidating learning, as described in Practice 3, also act to support the learning of students, whatever the classroom grouping.

A key issue here is for schools to use data to evaluate their current grouping practices. If, for example, part of the rationale of a particular grouping routine is to improve the learning of students experiencing difficulty, that will be evident in data available in normed assessments and growth within NAPLAN results.

PRACTICE 5

Teacher professional learning that focuses on classroom culture

Readers may be thinking that posing challenging tasks, structuring lessons around those tasks, and developing sequences of tasks and lessons makes sense, but are concerned about the willingness of students to take up the challenges, to listen to other students, and to engage with the learning sequences.

This section discusses the importance of professional learning around creating a classroom culture in which the expectation is that students will engage. The section is more general in nature than the previous sections in this book, as the ideas apply whatever the subject and whatever the approach to learning.

Embracing challenges consistently

Creating a classroom culture in which the expectation is that students will engage includes an anticipation that:

> tasks will be challenging

> lessons will be structured in particular ways, allowing students time to work on the task either by themselves or in small groups

> students will work on sequences of tasks, rather than one-off problems.

Further, these ways of working are not intended to be every now and again, but applied consistently. As the National Council of Teachers of Mathematics (NCTM 2014) notes:

> *Student learning is greatest in classrooms where the tasks consistently encourage high-level student thinking and reasoning and least in classrooms where the tasks are routinely procedural in nature. (p. 17)*

However, the key issue is the stance that students take, and their willingness to engage with the learning that such approaches offer. Key to this stance is what Dweck (2000) describes as a 'growth mindset', in which students believe they can get smarter by trying hard and being willing to embrace challenges.

Students with growth mindsets have specific traits. They:

> embrace challenges

> do not see difficulties they experience or mistakes as threats to their self-esteem

> keep trying even if the task they are working on is difficult.

Students with fixed mindsets—sometimes described as having a performance orientation—are concerned if they feel they might make a mistake and so look deficient in the eyes of the teacher, and so give up quickly. Such students prefer to do nothing rather than possibly make mistakes.

Of course, many students have a mix of mindsets, and possibly have different mindsets for different learning domains. For example, a student might have a growth mindset in sport but a fixed mindset when learning mathematics.

The role of disposition as either an enabler or inhibitor is widely known. On the morning of writing this, I read an article 'The biggest myth about math', by Sarah D. Sparks (2020), in which she concludes:

> *There aren't 'math people' and 'non-math people', only those who work through the challenging lesson and those who surrender too soon. Helping children understand that math doesn't define them, but can help them redefine their world, could be key to turning math anxiety into joy.*

The key issue is that teachers can change students' mindsets. Teachers do this by:

> the things they affirm—effort, persistence, cooperation, learning from others, flexible thinking

> the ways they affirm, and

> the types of classroom experiences they offer.

While it is possible for teachers to support students with fixed mindsets to develop growth mindsets, the opposite can also happen. For example, if classrooms are predominantly teacher-directed, this gives students the impression that their task is to follow the instructions closely, which can create anxiety and make mathematics learning high-risk. Likewise, if the classroom culture is one of competition, and if assessment is mainly comparing students against each other, this can move students with a growth mindset to be more performance oriented. This book is arguing that the majority of assessments should be formative and non-competitive.

Norms of activity

Also central to classroom culture are the norms of activity in mathematics classrooms. These mathematical norms include the principles, generalisations, processes and products that form the basis of the mathematics curriculum, broadly defined, and serve as the tools for other learning. The socio-mathematical norms encompass not only 'classroom actions and interactions that are specifically mathematical' (Cobb & McClain 1999, p. 219), but also the goals of interaction that address elements such as culture, social group, language comprehension and usage, and classroom organisation, as they relate to the teaching and learning of mathematics. Examples of such norms are that students are encouraged to listen to each other, and the teacher models the process of taking risks.

Another key example of these norms is the expectation that students will make a start on problems without direct interactions with the teacher. To support this, teachers can establish ways of structuring student responses. For example, older students can be encouraged to write what they currently know at the top of a page, to have rough working space under that, and to write a clear synthesised and systematic response to the task below that again. This is not always possible with younger students, but finding ways for them to record answers is clearly important.

Another approach might be to establish a class code, such as '4 before me' outlined earlier (see p. 48), which sets out four defined steps that students take before asking questions of the teacher. Yet another strategy is to inform students of a 'zone of confusion', or 'learning pit', into which *all* students go for some time and can only emerge with persistence and effort. In practice, it seems that the main beneficiaries of this zone or pit are students who usually think they are the only ones struggling.

In other words, this positive classroom culture is a product of:

> the type of task posed—if the tasks are too easy, students do not learn to persist

> the pedagogies used—if the teacher tells students how to solve a problem before they have had a chance to puzzle on it for themselves, there is no cognitive activation

> the fostering of student discussion of solutions, involving reasoning and argumentation

> student success being measured against criteria, rather than against other students.

Social interactions

In the end, classroom culture is about social relationships. Lerman (1998, p. 70) emphasises 'the centrality of the social relationships constituted and negotiated during classroom learning'. In clarifying this social perspective, Lerman elaborates on Vygotsky's (1978) 'zone of proximal development' (ZPD) metaphor. Lerman argues that 'the ZPD is created in the learning activity, which is a product of the task, the texts, the previous networks of experiences of the participants, the power relationships in the classroom, etc.' (p. 71). Even though the ZPD is sometimes used to describe teacher choice of an activity to allow students to step onto the next rung on a ladder of many miniscule steps of mathematics learning, Lerman argues that the ZPD is connected to creating classroom environments with conditions that are likely to facilitate student engagement in tasks.

The proposition is that learning is facilitated when students interact, both verbally and through made, drawn or written representations, both with each other and with the teacher. This creates a challenge for teachers, in that they ideally value the opinions of students and are not threatened by them. There is also a challenge for students to learn to listen to each other and to see learning as a collaborative venture—not a competitive one.

Summary and implications for professional learning

In summary, specific actions are needed to encourage all students to see that challenge and confusion can be part of learning. Indeed, if they are not being challenged, they are unlikely to be learning.

There is currently considerable attention given to the notion of growth mindsets across all education systems, and the ways that growth mindsets assist in mathematics learning should be the focus of classroom lessons, ideally at the start of the year.

Given that problems cannot be solved if the student does not start, teachers could discuss ways they have found to encourage students to get started. Likewise, students need to persist, even if the task is difficult. It can help this process if lessons are structured to encourage students to continue persisting. This includes an openness to learning from each other.

Teacher professional learning can focus on various strategies for:

› engaging students in their own learning

› creating classroom environments in which persistence and resilience are expected

› communicating with students about their role in their own learning.

But perhaps most important of all is finding ways to reduce the sense of risk that some students experience in mathematics classrooms.

PRACTICE 6

Improving learning through supported collaborative planning processes

It is now common that teachers—in primary schools, at least—are released from their classrooms to allow meaningful time to plan. The imperative then is to find ways to support teachers in maximising benefits from their collaborative planning. The discussion of this practice draws on two research-based models of teacher planning that can be used by schools and planning teams to structure meetings held for that purpose. Creating this planning time represents a significant investment for schools, so it makes sense to maximise its effectiveness.

There is a further advantage of collaborative planning that relates to teacher knowledge of mathematics and its teaching. It is assumed that reflective practitioners continue their learning for all of their careers. The hope is that teachers are still learning in their tenth, twentieth and thirtieth years of teaching. Collaborative planning is an obvious way of facilitating that teacher learning. There are quite a few opportunities for teachers to learn aspects of mathematics with which they are unfamiliar. Supportive, collaborative school-based teams are a non-threatening environment in which teachers can ask of others: 'Please explain that to me again.' Senior secondary mathematics teachers know they have to continue learning new approaches and new aspects of mathematics as the curriculum changes. Collaborative planning can support all teachers in learning new mathematics.

There are at least three levels of teacher planning:

> for the year

> for a unit—a sequence of lessons with a coherent focus, sometimes referred to as a topic sequence

> for a lesson.

The research literature has largely focused on planning at the level of the lesson. Indeed, articles on planning from the US commonly focus on implementing particular teaching pedagogies and activities. For example, Superfine (2008) notes that 'planning commonly refers to the time teachers spend preparing and designing activities for students' (p. 11).

Planning assumptions

The assumption is that planning informs teacher practice. All levels of the planning of mathematics teaching are important, from the sequencing of content and the structuring of lessons to the selection and preparation of materials and worksheets, as well as how teachers document their planning of lesson sequences or units of work.

A further assumption around this practice relates to documentation. Planning documents act as:

> a record of planning sessions

> a guide to an individual teacher's planning, such as their lessons

> a prompt for reflection.

One of the key aspects of planning documentation is the notion that planning is cumulative. In other words, the planning we did last year informs our plans this year and, along with our reflections, can be the start of our planning with a similar focus next year.

There appears to be a widespread belief in Australia that scripted units or lessons produced by commercial publishers or state and territory curriculum authorities are unlikely to facilitate the type of teacher decision-making that can lead to quality teaching (Sullivan, Clarke, Clarke, Farrell & Gerard 2013). Indeed, the national professional standards for Australian teachers (Australian Institute for Teaching and School Leadership 2015), under Standard 2.3 'Curriculum, assessment and reporting', at the lowest of four levels (Graduate), expect that teachers will 'use curriculum, assessment and reporting knowledge to design learning sequences and lesson plans' (p. 10). The emphasis in the standards on the role of assessment resonates with Sullivan et al. (2013).

Collaborative planning informed by research

It is assumed that teachers, when collaboratively planning, share ideas but then adapt those ideas to the local context. Roche, Clarke, Clarke and Sullivan (2014) analysed 48 unit programs from various schools and levels. While the programs varied in format and style, they summarise the common features of the documents of a unit as including:

> explicit identification of the content descriptions and proficiencies of the Australian Curriculum being addressed

> articulation of the key mathematical ideas that are inherent in the goals for the unit

> indication of prerequisite and new language and terminology associated with the unit

> suggestions of the focus for individual lessons that make up the unit, including particular tasks and activities that might form the basis of the lessons

> resources that can support the teaching of the lessons

> an indicative order of the lessons

> information about assessment tools, including strategies that inform learning.

Further elements that can enhance planning include:

> cross-curricula connections

> teacher reflections.

This is not intended as a checklist, but as a set of suggestions of aspects that can be considered in planning sessions and in the subsequent documentation. A key initial step for a planning team is to decide what aspects they will seek to address each time they plan, and the ways that they will document their planning. It is noted that there are advantages in having some commonality in planning process and documentation across a school. However, it is not important whether one school uses the same processes as another.

In exploring the processes that lead up to documentation, Sullivan, Clarke, Clarke, Gould, Leigh-Lancaster and Lewis (2012) surveyed over 600 teachers using fixed- and free-format items to seek insights into planning processes in mathematics. The responses were analysed to identify themes and common actions. They found little difference between the planning of primary and secondary teachers, although the planning of numeracy was different from literacy. The authors propose a framework for teacher unit planning (see Figure 6.1) that can be used as a guide to key planning processes. The framework assumes that a plan for the year has been established earlier (as indicated by the top arrows), and refers to the various actions in planning a unit.

Figure 6.1 A proposed framework for teacher planning based on focus group and survey data

```
↓                    ↓                    ↓                    ↓
Checking         Examining            Drawing on          Drawing on
school or web    curriculum           experience (self    assessment
documents,   ↔   content          ↔   and colleagues) ↔   of student
teacher          descriptions                             readiness
resources and/or to identify the
student texts    important idea(s)

              → Establishing specific learning goals ←
                              ↓
              Selecting and sequencing
              tasks including adapting them
              for your students
                              ↓
              Planning the teaching and
              assessment, including differentiating
              for particular students
                              ↓
```

Improving learning through supported collaborative planning processes

It is assumed that this model applies to the teaching of aspects of mathematical content such as fractions or geometry at a given level, rather than something more general such as 'costs of travel'. The first pair of boxes on the top line (checking resources; examining curriculum content), act together and interact. Likewise, the second pair of boxes on the top line (drawing on experience; drawing on assessment) also interact. In terms of processes, it is proposed that planning teams explicitly attend to each aspect represented by a box in the diagram. So, focus questions that are specifically addressed in planning sessions might be:

> What does the curriculum suggest?
> What resources do we have access to?
> What are our favourite suggestions for teaching this?
> What do our students know, and what do they find difficult?

The next step is to define specific learning goals, then to list and sequence the tasks and lessons, then to plan lessons—especially ways in which the learning can be differentiated to cater for all students. At this stage, it is also useful to plan how the learning will be assessed.

The intention would be to use a similar structure to inform the planning of all learning sequences. This assists in preparation for the planning meetings, as teachers can become familiar with the usual focuses for discussion and can prepare in advance resources and evidence that can be used to inform planning.

Davidson (2019) elaborates this framework in her doctorate in which she draws on data from surveys of groups of teachers and intensive case studies. Her model is presented in Figure 6.2.

Figure 6.2 Model of the processes and stages of planning and evaluating mathematics teaching

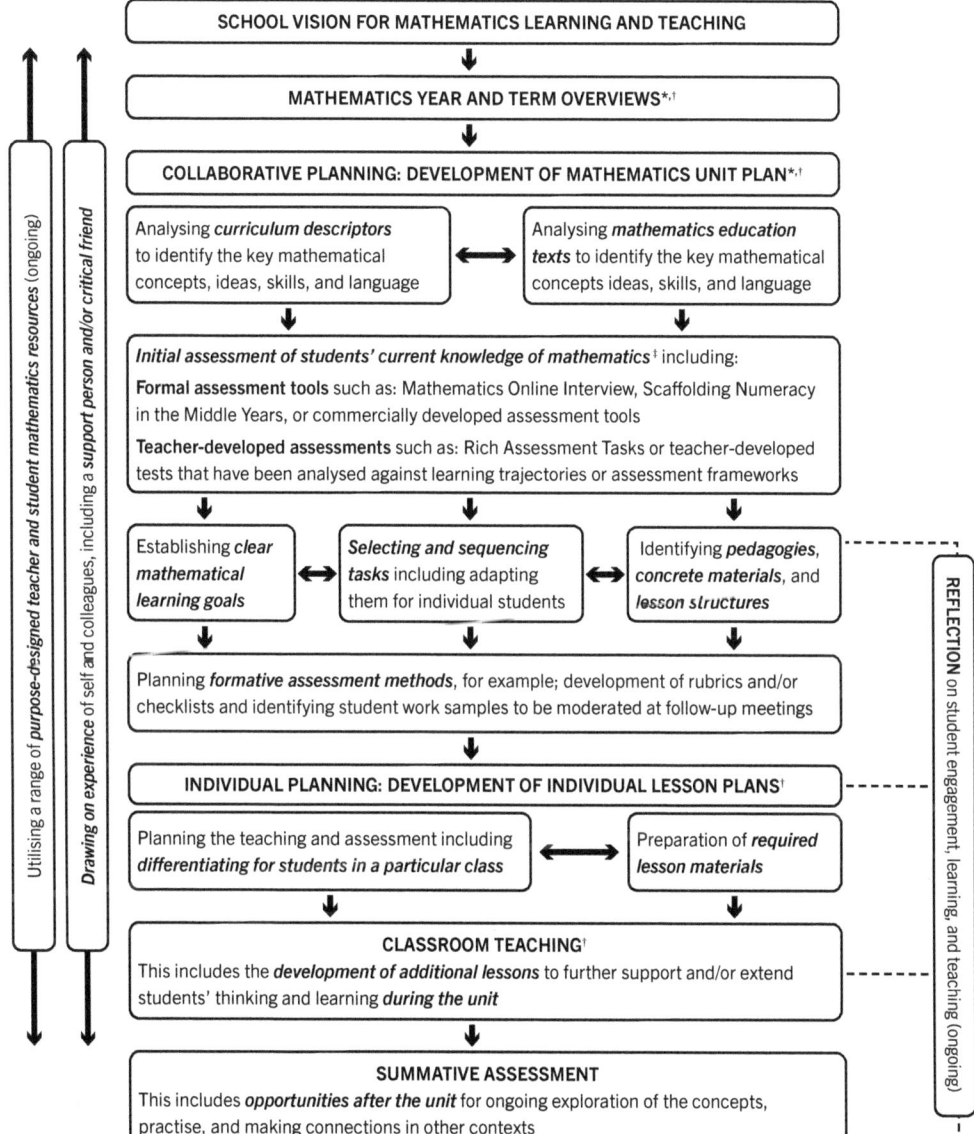

* Year and term overviews depict a learning trajectory that reflects key mathematical concepts and curriculum expectations, highlights the potential for developing interconnected mathematical concepts, and identifies cross-curricular learning opportunities.

† Overviews, unit and lesson plans are flexible in the time allocated to teach and respond to student learning needs.

‡ Initial assessments are developed and administered in a timely manner to inform the planning of a unit of work

Source: Adapted from Davidson 2019.

The schematic can also be used to guide collaborative planning processes and provide a structure for planning sessions. Davidson's schematic emphasises complementary planning undertaken by individual teachers after the team-planning sessions.

Summary and implications for professional learning

Practice 6 proposes specific models to guide and structure teacher collaborative planning. It assumes that school routines include times for such planning, and that school leadership takes an active role in supporting such planning. This involves structuring meetings, as well as determining streamlined templates for documenting planning, while noting that templates have the potential to be burdensome rather than helpful. Certainly standardising formats allows easier communication across school levels and across years. It is also important to have systems for filing plans so that the planning in year x is informed by planning and reflection on the plans from year x – 1 and, in turn, can inform planning in year x + 1.

School leaders clearly have a critical role in this. This includes:

> creating time for teachers to meet

> providing locations for such meetings that minimise interruptions

> establishing expectations for conduct of the meetings and the documentation

> encouraging discussions on the transfer of planning process to classroom actions.

There is no better way for leaders to show the importance of collaborative planning than to attend planning meetings—and to spend most of the time listening.

The evidence of success of planning processes is in the nature of the documentation, fidelity of individual teachers to the collaboratively developed plans, and even feedback from teachers on the extent to which they find the templates supportive and the plans from previous years accessible.

PRACTICE 7

Professional learning focusing on six principles of effective mathematics teaching

Practice 7 draws on research findings and other sets of recommendations for teaching actions. It presents a set of six principles that can guide teaching practice and teacher professional learning. There is some overlap with the content of earlier practices, and—as these principles form a coherent whole—some content is repeated. There are obvious connections with the HITS.

The six principles for teaching mathematics draw on particular national and international research reviews and summaries of recommendations about mathematics teaching. For example, the six principles for teaching mathematics incorporate key ideas from an early set of recommendations for mathematics teaching by Good, Grouws and Ebmeier (1983), who synthesised results related to the effective teaching literature of the time. The principles also draw on Hattie (2009), who analysed a large number of studies that provide evidence about correlates of student achievement. He reports the effect size of a wide range of variables related to teachers, class grouping and teaching practices, noting that identifying higher effect sizes is important since almost any intervention results in some improvement.

The six principles are also based on recommendations from Swan (2005), who presents a range of important suggestions—derived from earlier studies of teacher learning and classroom practice—on how teaching could move from promoting passive learning to promoting active learning, and from transmissive to connected and challenging teaching. Clarke and Clarke (2004) have developed a similar set of recommendations, arising from detailed case studies of teachers who had been identified as particularly effective in the Australian 'Early numeracy research project'. Their list is grouped under 10 headings and 25 specific actions. While their list is drawn from research with Early Years mathematics teachers, the headings and actions listed are applicable at all levels. Anthony and Walshaw's (2009) detailed best-evidence synthesis is also used. Anthony and Walshaw reviewed important research on mathematics teaching and learning—from the research, they produced a list of ten pedagogies, which they argue are important for mathematics teaching.

The following text presents the six principles, along with some indication of the impetus for each principle, written in the form of advice to teachers.

Principle 1: Setting goals

Principle 1 is elaborated for teachers as follows:

> Identify key ideas that underpin the concepts you are seeking to teach, communicate to students that these are the goals of the teaching, and

explain to them how you hope they will learn.

Principle 1 emphasises the importance of the teacher having clear and explicit goals that are connected to the pedagogical approach they have chosen to assist students in learning. One of the main recommendations by Hattie (2009), which had been earlier elaborated in Hattie and Timperley (2007), is that feedback is one of the main influences on student achievement. The key elements of feedback are for students to receive information on 'Where am I going?', 'How am I going?', and 'Where am I going to next?' Feedback is one of the HITS (Department of Education and Training 2017) that has not been explicitly mentioned earlier in this book. Feedback is described as informing:

> *a student and/or teacher about the student's performance relative to learning goals. Feedback redirects or refocuses teacher and student actions so the student can align effort and activity with a clear outcome that leads to achieving a learning goal. Teachers and peers can provide formal or informal feedback. It can be oral, written, formative or summative. Whatever its form, it comprises specific advice a student can use to improve performance. (p. 9)*

Supporting students towards achieving the goals and making decisions on pathways to achieving the intentions interactively requires teachers to have clear aspirations for the learning. This is what Swan (2005) describes as 'making the purposes of activities clear' (p. 6), and what Clarke and Clarke (2004) propose as the need to 'focus on important mathematical ideas and make the mathematical focus clear to the children' (p. 68).

Principle 1 also reflects one of the key goals in the presentation and content descriptions of Australian Curriculum: Mathematics. ACARA (2009) argues for the centrality of teacher decision-making, with the curriculum being written to be deliberately succinct and specific, so that teachers can make active judgements on the emphases in their teaching. The flexibility in the modes of presentation of the content descriptions also indicates to teachers that their first step in planning their teaching is to make active decisions about their focus, and to communicate that focus to the students.

In particular, according to the thinking underpinning Principle 1, it is assumed that teachers would specifically plan the key ideas or concepts to be addressed in the lesson before students begin. It is also expected that the students will learn, through working on a task, listening to the explanations of others, or by practising mathematical techniques. In most lessons, these intentions would be made clear to the students, although it is essential that the intentions do not reduce the possibility of students thinking for themselves. Similarly, it is important that establishing criteria for success does not exclude some students from the possibility of achievement, while also setting the bar too low for others.

Principle 2: Making connections

Principle 2 is elaborated for teachers as follows:

> Build on what students know, mathematically and experientially, including creating and connecting students with stories that both contextualise and establish a rationale for the learning.

One aspect of Principle 2 is the importance of practical mathematics and numeracy. The following example of making tasks relevant is drawn from a suggestion by one of the teachers in the 'Maths in the Kimberley' project (Jorgensen, Sullivan & Grootenboer 2013). A commonly used mathematics problem at middle primary levels is posed as follows:

A farmyard has pigs and chickens. There are 10 heads and 26 legs. How many pigs and chickens might there be?

The task is interesting, as can it be solved by:

> guess and check

> drawing diagrams, or

> formal algebraic methods.

Perhaps the power of the task lies in contrasting the different methods. But the task, as posed, may not be suitable for students who are unfamiliar with farmyard contexts. In the project, one of the teachers suggested the following formulation for her Aboriginal students being educated in the Kimberly region:

A truck has some people and some dogs in the back. There are 10 heads and 26 legs. How many people and how many dogs are there?

The problem and the mathematical potential are the same but the context is different, while the word changes make the context more appropriate for the teacher's students.

A second aspect of Principle 2 relates to using assessment information to inform teaching. Hattie (2009) and Swan (2005) both argue for the constructive use of students' prior knowledge and, to obtain this, teachers need to assess what their students know and can do. Clarke and Clarke (2004) recommend that teachers build connections from prior lessons and experiences and use data effectively to inform learning. Anthony and Walshaw (2009) emphasise building on student experience and thinking. A key issue in this is using data to inform teaching decisions. While it is unfortunate that NAPLAN results are often used to facilitate cross-school comparisons, the analysis of facilities of individual items and groups of items can be used to inform planning and teaching.

Principle 3: Fostering engagement

Principle 3 is elaborated for teachers as follows:

> Engage students by utilising a variety of rich and challenging tasks that allow students time and opportunities to make decisions, and which use a variety of forms of representation.

Principle 3 is fundamentally about seeking to make mathematics learning engaging for students. This is the same argument that is presented in Practice 1.

Swan (2005) emphasises the importance of challenging student thinking through questioning; Good et al. (1983) recommend the use of higher order questions; Clarke and Clarke (2004) suggest using a range of practical contexts and representations having high expectations; and Anthony and Walshaw (2009) argue it is critical that teachers use 'worthwhile tasks' that are meaningful and relevant to students. Implementing this principle may be confronting for some mathematics teachers, and these strategies can effectively become the focus of teacher learning.

Principle 4: Differentiating challenges

Principle 4 is elaborated for teachers as follows:

> Interact with students while they engage in the experiences, encourage students to interact with each other, including asking and answering questions, and specifically plan to support students who need it and challenge those who are ready.

Principle 4 is fundamentally about differentiating student support according to the different needs of individual students. This is directly related to the content presented in Practice 4. It is also about the overall vision of what constitutes an effective classroom dynamic and structure. As argued previously, students are more likely to feel included in the work of the class, and to experience success, if teachers offer *enabling* prompts to allow those experiencing difficulty to engage in active experiences related to the initial goal task, rather than, for example, requiring such students to listen to additional explanations, or assuming that they will pursue goals substantially different from the rest of the class.

Likewise, students who complete the work quickly can be posed *extending* prompts that challenge their thinking, within the context of the original task. Enabling and extending prompts were elaborated upon earlier, and examples of the types of tasks were given, especially those with low floors and high ceilings—including open-ended tasks, which are the tasks most suited to the creation of such prompts.

Principle 5: Structuring lessons

Principle 5 is elaborated for teachers as follows:

> Adopt pedagogies that foster communication and both individual and group responsibilities, use students' reports to the class as learning opportunities, with teacher summaries elaborating key mathematical ideas.

Principle 5 is essentially advice about the structuring of lessons, and connects with Practice 2. There is a lesson format that is commonly recommended to Australian teachers which, in summary, is described as: launch, explore, summarise, review.

A different perspective on this guideline can be gained from the Japanese way of describing the structure of their lessons. For example, Inoue (2010, p. 6) uses four terms: *hatsumon, kikanjyuski, nerige* and *matome*, which are explained as follows:

> *Hatsumon* means the posing of the initial problem that will form the basis of the lesson, and the articulation to students of what it is intended that they learn.

> *Kikanjyuski* involves individual or group work on the problem. The intention is that all students have the opportunity to work individually so that when there is an opportunity to communicate with other students they have something to say. There is a related aspect to this described as *kikanshido* that describes the teacher thoughtfully walking around the desks giving feedback and making observations that can inform subsequent phases in the lesson.

> *Nerige* refers to carefully managed whole-class discussion seeking the students' insights. There is an

> explicit expectation that students, when reporting on their work, communicate with other students.

> *Matome* refers to the teacher summary of the key ideas.

The last two steps are perhaps the least practised by Australian mathematics teachers—yet they are critical for the implementation of structured student-centred approaches to inquiry.

There is an assumption in this Japanese lesson structure, and also in principles 3 and 4, that students will engage in learning experiences in which they have had the opportunity for creative and constructive thinking. This Japanese lesson structure assumes that all students have participated in common activities and shared experiences that are both social and mathematical, and that an element of their learning is connected to opportunities to report the products of their experience to others, and to also hear others' reports.

For the mathematical aspects, it is argued that students can benefit from either giving or listening to explanations of strategies or results, and that this can best be done along with the rest of the class with the teacher participating, especially facilitating and emphasising mathematical communication and justification. A key element of this style of teaching and learning is giving students the opportunity to see the variability in responses (Watson & Sullivan 2008), as confirming this variability can consolidate underlying concepts for students.

Another aspect of reviews at the end of lessons is the contribution they make to social learning. This is related to a sense of belonging to a classroom community, and is also connected to building awareness of differences between students and acceptance of these differences. Such differences can be a product of students':

> prior mathematical experiences

> familiarity with classroom processes (Delpit 1988)

- social, cultural and linguistic backgrounds (Zevenbergen 2000)
- motivation (Middleton 1995)
- persistence and efficacy (Dweck 2000), as well as a range of other factors.

Principle 6: Promoting fluency and transfer

Principle 6 is elaborated for teachers as follows:

> Fluency is important, and it can be developed in two ways: by short everyday practice of mental processes; and by practice, reinforcement and prompting transfer of learnt skills.

Principle 6 is familiar to most mathematics teachers, but it is possible to misinterpret the purpose of practice and prompting transfer. Skemp (1986) contrasts mechanical with automatic skills practice. With mechanical practice, students have limited capacity to adapt the learnt skill to other situations. With automatic practice, built on understanding, students can be procedurally fluent while at the same time having conceptual understanding. Likewise, the importance of prompting mathematical knowledge transfer is clearly argued by Bransford et al. (1999), and the importance of this for learners' future lives is mentioned in Practice 2.

Summary and implications for professional learning

In summary, this practice presented a synthesis of research recommendations via its six principles for teaching mathematics, which can be used both individually and collectively. As a group, the set of six principles unify the key ideas elaborated in various practices of this book.

Conclusion

This book is intended to inform school leadership teams, especially principals, on important aspects of mathematics and numeracy teaching and, in particular, on potential emphases for teacher professional learning. Of course, the suggestions are too comprehensive to be enacted in a single year, but plans can be developed for cumulative and progressive implementation over time.

In all cases, the interaction of factors influencing planning and teaching of mathematics described by Sullivan, Borcek, Walker and Rennie (2016) can guide evaluation of progress and improvement. As implied in the model, teacher knowledge about mathematics and pedagogy influence—and are influenced by—teacher dispositions about mathematics and learning, as well as the opportunities and constraints that are anticipated. These act together to inform teachers' intentions—meaning their planning—which then influence their classroom actions. This is where improvement can be noticed and the actions then impact on the rest of the model in a cyclic and iterative process.

This book presents the details of seven particular practices that have been, in turn, connected to particular HITS. The following paragraphs elaborate upon those connections.

Setting goals

Setting goals refers to the intentions of the teacher for the learning of the students. Setting goals connects direct to the E2030 aspects described as *focus* and *choice*. The set goals can be on aspects of content, as elaborated in curriculum documents, for example, or ways of enacting mathematics, which are described in the Australian Curriculum as proficiencies.

Clearly structured student-centred inquiry can only be successful if the teachers are aware of the specific goals of the learning. It is sometimes useful for teachers to explicitly communicate these goals to students. This process is often described as 'writing learning intentions'. It is often recommended that teachers also indicate to students actions that could constitute success. In some cases that is helpful. However, in other cases, articulating specific criteria for success can have the effect of setting goals too high for some students and too low for others, so it is recommended that care be taken when communicating learning intentions and success criteria to students.

Structuring lessons

Structuring lessons refers to elements that together constitute the lesson. As described in Practice 2, there is no one structure that applies to all aspects of learning mathematics—or anything else—but it is important for teachers to make active decisions on the structure they intend to use for any one lesson. There are, of course, elements in common with the various structures elaborated in Practice 2.

Explicit teaching

Explicit teaching is sometimes taken to refer to information and directions from the teacher that is intended to guide students' thinking and response. As I argue in Practice 1 and Practice 2, 'teaching telling' is hardly ever productive for mathematics learning. However, after students have engaged in structured inquiry—and discussed their insights from that inquiry—it is important that teachers actively synthesise students' thinking. A more productive time for teacher instruction is *after* students have had a learning experience.

Worked examples

The phrase 'worked examples' is sometimes taken to mean the process in most mathematics textbooks in which specific solutions are given for exercises and problems that are in the subsequent set. Such worked examples may be useful at times. But active sharing of student-generated solutions is more productive. There are hardly any mathematics problems—at least at primary and secondary level— that can only be solved one way, so insisting that students solve problems in ways suggested by the teacher is potentially limiting and counterproductive.

Collaborative learning

Collaborative learning aligns with the overall recommended approaches in this book, as this pedagogical approach puts students' thinking at the centre. The 'Think, pair, share' approach is useful for this:

> All students are given time to think at the start of an inquiry.

> Students then discuss their insights in a very small group, and investigate further.

> The resulting insights can then be discussed with larger groups or the whole class.

Multiple exposures

Multiple exposures aligns with Practice 3 on sequence and with what E2030 describes as 'alignment'. Most structured inquiries activate students' cognition. There is almost always a need for consolidation of learning through further experiences that can be described as 'a bit the same and a bit different'.

Questioning and feedback

Questioning and feedback refer to interactions with the students, and they go together. Listening is perhaps more important than questioning. The process, which occurs interactively, is that teachers listen to students or read their written products, ask further questions, and then provide feedback on the alignment of student thinking with the intended learning and the appropriateness of that thinking.

Metacognitive strategies

Metacognitive strategies are about helping students to rise above the specific examples to consider the whole in which the specific experiences are set. Student-created topic summaries can be used for this, as can student reflective journals and specific prompts. For example, if students are working through a set of practice exercises, it is possible to ask questions to encourage students to consider the overall intent, such as, 'In what ways is Question 2 different from (or the same as) Question 1?'

Differentiated teaching

Differentiated teaching is perhaps the most important of all of the HITS, and aligns with the general equity focus of the E2030 initiative. As described in Practice 4, one important goal of education is to foster an inclusive world that graduating students feel a part of. Unfortunately, mathematics teaching often has the effect of alienating some students, resulting in them feeling excluded. It is argued that pedagogies—and particularly grouping practices—should ensure that all students have maximum opportunity to learn mathematics. More than any of the other practices presented in this book, school leadership teams should gather ongoing evidence on the extent to which their attempts at inclusion through differentiated teaching are effective.

Like more or less all educational improvement initiatives, improvement in mathematics and numeracy teaching and learning is a journey, rather than a destination.

REFERENCES

ACARA 2009, *The shape of the Australian Curriculum: mathematics*, http://www.acara.edu.au/verve/_resources/Australian_Curriculum_-_Maths.pdf

ACARA 2012, *The shape of the Australian Curriculum*, http://www.acara.edu.au/verve/_resources/The_Shape_of_the_Australian_Curriculum_V3.pdf

Alfieri, L, Brooks, PJ, Aldrich, NJ, & Tenenbaum, HR 2011, 'Does discovery-based instruction enhance learning?', *Journal of Educational Psychology*, vol. 103, no. 1, pp. 1–18.

Anthony, G, & Walshaw, M 2009, *Effective pedagogy in mathematics,* Educational series 19, International Academy of Education, Brussels & Geneva.

Australian Institute for Teaching and School Leadership 2015, *Australian professional standards for teachers*, AITSL, Canberra.

Bransford, JB, Brown, AL, & Cocking, RR (eds) 1999, *How people learn: brain, mind, experience, and school,* Committee on Developments in the Science of Learning, National Research Council, London.

Brophy, JE 1983, 'Research on the self-fulfilling prophecy and teacher expectations', *Journal of Educational Psychology*, vol. 75, no. 5, pp. 631–61.

Christiansen, B, & Walther, G 1986, *Task and activity*, in B Christiansen, AG Howson, & M Otte (eds), *Perspectives on mathematics education*, pp. 243–307, Reidel, Dordrecht.

Clarke, DM, & Clarke, BA 2004, 'Mathematics teaching in Grades K–2: painting a picture of challenging, supportive, and effective classrooms', in RN Rubenstein & GW Bright (eds), *Perspectives on the teaching of mathematics*, 66th Yearbook of the National Council of Teachers of Mathematics, pp. 67–81, NCTM, Reston, VA.

Cobb, P, & McClain, K 1999, 'Supporting teachers' learning in social and institutional context', in Fou-Lai Lin (ed.), *Proceedings of the 1999 International Conference on Mathematics Teacher Education* (pp. 7–77), National Taiwan Normal University, Taipei.

Davidson, A 2019, 'Investigating primary teachers' mathematics planning processes for student-centred learning and teaching', doctoral dissertation, Monash University, Australia.

Delpit, L 1988, 'The silenced dialogue: power and pedagogy in educating other people's children', *Harvard Educational Review,* vol. 58, no. 3, pp. 280–98.

Department of Education and Training 2017, *High impact teaching strategies*, Department of Education and Training, Melbourne, https://www.education.vic.gov.au/school/teachers/teachingresources/practice/improve/Pages/hits.aspx

Desforges, C, & Cockburn, A 1987, *Understanding the mathematics teacher: a study of practice in first schools*, Palmer Press, London.

Doyle, W 1986, 'Classroom organisation and management', in MC Wittrock (ed.), *Handbook of research on teaching*, pp. 392–431, Macmillan, New York.

Dreyfus, T, & Tsamir, P 2004, 'Ben's consolidation of knowledge structures about infinite sets', *The Journal of Mathematical Behavior*, vol. 23, no. 3, pp. 271–300.

Dweck, CS 2000, *Self theories: their role in motivation, personality, and development*, Psychology Press, Philadelphia.

Elliot, AJ 1999, 'Approach and avoidance motivation and achievement goals', *Educational Psychologist*, vol. 34, no. 3, pp. 169–89.

Fredericks, JA, Blumfield, PC, & Paris, AH 2004, 'School engagement: potential of the concept, state of the evidence', *Review of Educational Research*, vol. 74, no. 1, pp. 59–110.

Good, TL, Grouws, DA, & Ebmeier, H 1983, *Active mathematics teaching*, Longman, New York.

Hattie, J 2009, *Visible learning: a synthesis of over 800 meta-analyses relating to achievement*, Routledge, London.

Hattie, J, & Timperley, H 2007, 'The power of feedback', *Review of Educational Research*, vol. 77, no. 1, pp. 81–112.

Inoue, N 2010, 'Zen and the art of neriage: Facilitating consensus building in mathematics inquiry lessons through lesson study', *Journal of Mathematics Teacher Education*, vol. 14, pp. 5–23, doi: 10.1007/s10857-010-9150-z

Jorgensen, R, Sullivan, P, & Grootenboer, P. (eds) 2013, *Pedagogies to enhance learning for Indigenous students*, Springer, New York.

Kilpatrick, J, Swafford, J, & Findell, B 2001, *Adding it up: how children learn mathematics*, National Research Council, Washington, DC.

Kullberg, A, Runesson, U, & Mårtensson, P 2013, 'The same task? Different learning possibilities', in C Margolinas (ed.), *Task design in mathematics education: proceedings of the International Commission on Mathematics Instruction Study 22*, pp. 609–16, ICMI, Oxford, UK.

Lerman, S 1998, 'A moment in the zoom of a lens: towards a discursive psychology of mathematics teaching and learning', in A Olivier & K Newstead (eds), *Proceedings of the 22nd Conference of the International Group for the Psychology of Mathematics Education*, vol. 1, pp. 66–81, Stellenbosch, South Africa.

Lovitt, C, & Clarke, D 1988, *Mathematics curriculum and teaching program: activity bank*, vols. 1 & 2, Curriculum Corporation, Canberra.

Marsh, HW, Craven, RG, & McInerney, D (eds) 2005, *New frontiers in SELF research*, Information Age Press, Greenwich, CT.

Martin, A, & Marsh, H 2006, 'Academic resilience and its psychological and educational correlates', *Psychology in Schools*, vol. 43, no. 3, pp. 267–81.

Masters, GN 2012, 'National school improvement tool', Australian Council for Educational Research, Camberwell, Vic, https://research.acer.edu.au/tll_misc/18/

Middleton, JA 1995, 'A study of intrinsic motivation in the mathematics classroom: a personal construct approach', *Journal for Research in Mathematics Education*, vol. 26, no. 3, pp. 254–79.

National Council of Teachers of Mathematics 2014, *Principles to action: Ensuring mathematics success for all*, NCTM, Reston, VA.

Organisation for Economic Co-operation and Development [OECD] 2016, *Key questions for mathematics teachers and how PISA can answer them,* slide 29, figure 2.2, OECD, Paris, https://www.slideshare.net/OECDEDU/key-questions-for-mathematics-teachers-and-how-pisa-can-answer-them

Organisation for Economic Co-operation and Development [OECD] 2019, *The future of education and skills: education 2030,* OECD, Paris, https://www.oecd.org/education/2030/E2030%20Position%20Paper%20(05.04.2018).pdf

Program for International Student Assessment [PISA] 2018, home page, PISA, Paris, http://www.oecd.org/pisa/

Russo, J 2015, 'How challenging tasks optimise cognitive load', in K Beswick, T Muir, & J Wells (eds), *Proceedings of 39th Psychology of Mathematics Education Conference,* vol. 4, pp. 105–12, PME, Hobart, Tas.

Russo, J, & Hopkins, S 2017, 'How does lesson structure shape teacher perceptions of teaching with challenging tasks?' *Mathematics Teacher Education and Development,* vol. 19, no. 1, pp. 30–46.

Roche, A, Clarke, DM, Clarke, J, & Sullivan, P 2014, 'Primary teachers' written unit plans in mathematics and their perceptions of essential elements of these', *Mathematics Education Research Journal,* vol. 26, no. 4, pp. 853–70.

Simon, M 1995, 'Reconstructing mathematics pedagogy from a constructivist perspective', *Journal for Research in Mathematics Education,* vol. 26, pp. 114–45.

Skemp, RR 1986, *The psychology of learning mathematics,* 2nd edn, Penguin, London.

Smith, MS, & Stein, MK 2011, *5 practices for orchestrating productive mathematical discussions,* National Council of Teachers of Mathematics, Reston, VA.

Sparks, SD 2020, 'The myth fueling math anxiety', *Education Week,* 7 January, https://www.edweek.org/ew/articles/2020/01/08/the-biggest-myth-about-math.html

Stein, MK, Grover, B, & Henningsen, M 1996, 'Building students' capacity for mathematical thinking and reasoning: an analysis of mathematical tasks used in reform classrooms', *American Educational Research Journal,* vol. 33, no. 2, pp. 455–88.

Sullivan, P 1999, 'Seeking a rationale for particular classroom tasks and activities', in JM Truran & KN Truran (eds), *Making the difference,* Proceedings of the 21st Conference of the Mathematics Educational Research Group of Australasia, pp. 15–29, MERGA, Adelaide.

Sullivan, P 2007, 'Creating mathematics lessons', in S Close, D Corcoran and T Dooley (eds), *Proceedings of the Second National Conference on Research in Mathematics Education,* pp. 30–43, Dublin.

Sullivan, P 2011, *Teaching mathematics: using research-informed strategies,* ACER Press, Camberwell, Vic, https://research.acer.edu.au/cgi/viewcontent.cgi?article=1022&context=aer

Sullivan, P 2015, 'Maximising opportunities in mathematics for all students: addressing within-school and within-class differences', in A Bishop, H Tan & T Barkatsas (eds), *Diversity in mathematics education: towards inclusive practices,* pp. 239–53, Springer, Netherlands.

Sullivan, P, Bobis, J, Downton, A, Livy, S, Hughes, S, McCormick, M, & Russo, J 2020, 'Ways that relentless consistency and task variation contribute to teacher and student mathematics learning', in A Coles (ed.), *For the Learning of Mathematics Monograph 1: Proceedings of a symposium on learning in honour of Laurinda Brown,* pp. 32–37, FLM Publishing Association, Canada.

Sullivan, P, Bobis, J, Downton, A, Livy, S, Russo, J, Stenning, P, & Giannopoulos, J 2019, 'Exploring mathematical sequences of connected cumulative challenging tasks', Catholic Education Melbourne, Vic.

Sullivan, P, Borcek, C, Walker, N, & Rennie, M 2016, 'Exploring a structure for mathematics lessons that initiate learning by activating cognition on challenging tasks', *Journal of Mathematical Behavior*, vol. 41, 159–70, http://doi.org/10.1016/j.jmathb.2015.12.002

Sullivan, P, Clarke, D, & Clarke, B 2013, *Teaching with tasks for effective mathematics learning*, Springer, New York.

Sullivan, P, Clarke, DJ, Clarke, DM, Farrell, L, & Gerrard, J 2013, 'Processes and priorities in planning mathematics teaching', *Mathematics Education Research Journal*, vol. 25, no. 4, pp. 457–80.

Sullivan, P, Clarke, D, Clarke, D, Gould, P, Leigh-Lancaster, D, & Lewis G 2012, 'Insights into ways that teachers plan their mathematics teaching', in J Dindyal, LP Cheng, & SF Ng (eds), *Mathematics education: expanding horizons,* Proceedings of the 35th Annual Conference of the Mathematics Education Research Group of Australasia, pp. 696–703, MERGA, Singapore.

Sullivan, P, Tobias, S, & McDonough, A 2006, 'Perhaps the decision of some students not to engage in learning mathematics in school is deliberate', *Educational Studies in Mathematics*, vol. 62, pp. 81–99.

Superfine, A 2008, 'Planning for mathematics instruction: a model of experienced teachers' planning processes in context of a reform mathematics curriculum', *The Mathematics Educator*, vol. 18, no. 2, pp. 11–22.

Swan, M n.d., 'Using percent to increase quantities', Standards Unit trial materials. UK.

Swan, M 2005, *Improving learning in mathematics: challenges and strategies*, Department of Education and Skills Standards Unity, Sheffield.

Thompson, S, De Bortoli, L, Nicholas, M, Hillman, K, & Buckley, S 2010, *Challenges for Australian education: results from PISA 2009*, Australian Council for Educational Research, Camberwell, Vic.

Vygotsky, LS 1978, *Mind in society: the development of higher psychological processes*, M Cole, V John-Steiner, S Scribner, & E Souberman (eds & trans.), Harvard University Press, Cambridge, MA.

Watson, A, & Sullivan, P 2008, 'Teachers learning about tasks and lessons', in D Tirosh, & T Wood (eds), *Tools and resources in mathematics teacher education*, pp. 109–35, Sense, Rotterdam.

Wiliam, D 2016, The 9 things every teacher should know, tes.com, https://www.tes.com/us/news/breaking-views/9-things-every-teacher-should-know

Wood, T 2005, 'From alternative epistemologies to practice in education: rethinking what it means to teach and learn', in LP Steffe & J Gale (eds), *Constructivism in education*, pp. 331–9, Lawrence Erlbaum Associates, Hillsdale, New Jersey.

Zevenbergen, R 2000, '"Cracking the code" of mathematics: school success as a function of linguistic, social and cultural background', in J Boaler (ed.), *Multiple perspectives on mathematics teaching and learning*, pp. 201–23, JAI/Ablex, New York.

www.ingramcontent.com/pod-product-compliance
Lightning Source LLC
Chambersburg PA
CBHW061126070526
44584CB00033B/4239